# FROM  TO DANCING

## GOD'S GRACE FOR THOSE STRUGGLING WITH PORNOGRAPHY

by Mike Novotny

NORTHWESTERN PUBLISHING HOUSE
Milwaukee, Wisconsin

Cover Illustrations: Shutterstock
Art Director: Karen Knutson
Designer: Pam Dunn

Northwestern Publishing House
1250 N. 113th St., Milwaukee, Wl 53226-3284
www.nph.net
© 2018 Northwestern Publishing House
Published 2018
Printed in the United States of America
ISBN 978-0-8100-2930-9
ISBN 978-0-8100-2931-6 (e-book)

23  24  25  26  27      10  9  8  7  6  5  4  3  2

# CONTENTS

**INTRODUCTION**

# From ꓓꕱꘜꕔꝐ to Dancing

It was a dirty thing to say. "I want your money, Dad, not you!" But that is what the son said. Convinced he would be happier with cold hard cash than with his warmhearted dad, the son dared to speak those dirty words to his father. Before Dad could even dry the tears from his cheeks or say goodbye, the son packed his things. The boy grinned in expectation as he turned his face toward a new adventure and turned his back on the one who loved him before the day he was born.

It was a dirty place to go. The corners where girls winked at plain-faced guys as if they were drop-dead handsome. But that is where the son went. Lipstick and neon lights drew him to the places where pleasure was for sale. And he was buying. One girl, then another, then he lost track of the number. And he lost track of their names. Who had time for trivial things like conversation when there were more intoxicating ideas to explore?

It was a dirty thing to do. Squander the dollars his dad worked so hard for. But that is what the son did. The bank statements saw it coming, but who had time to open the mail when girls were begging for your attention? One day, his stash felt a little light. Opening the bag of coins his father had given him, the son rummaged around the empty wrappers and found . . . nothing. Not a drachma left. Broker than an umbrella salesman during a drought. Squandered every shekel on the kind of women his father warned him about.

It was a dirty job to take. Slopping slop into a filthy trough. But that is the job the son took. Terrible hours and terrible odors, but starvation has a way of making you settle. As the pigs oinked, his stomach ached. Ached for a spoonful of the slop the hogs were inhaling. At the same time, his heart ached over something else. Over what he had said and where he had gone and what he had done. Over the mess he had made. Over his sin.

But that was the very moment when the lightbulb went on— the first sensible thought he had thought in forever. "I could go home . . . " Well, not "home." The son knew better than that. He burned that bridge when he spit in his father's face and left the family for girls and goblets of wine. He was too dirty to be called a son. His sandal-less feet were filthy, but not nearly as filthy as his conscience. But maybe a dirty guy like him could work in the dirty fields, getting his hands and feet dirty with a hard day's work for a hard day's pay. That was the plan. From dirty to duty.

What the son never expected was that by the end of the day, he would go from dirty to dancing.

But dance he did. The dance steps started on the road that led home. His father saw him from a distance (was he watching and waiting that whole time?) and flew off the back porch, not a dirty look to be seen in his eyes. Before the son could say a word, the dance began, a slow dance of forgiveness. Wrapping his arms around the boy's dirty neck, the father swayed back and forth, rocking him like a child, kissing him on every silent beat.

Before the boy knew it, the actual music was playing, a beat so infectious that even Pharisees would have tapped their toes. His father practically dragged him out to the dance floor, spinning him so fast the son's laundry-fresh robe whirled up to his knees. Roaring with laughter, his father wrapped an arm around his shoulders and started a father-son kick line, showing off the boy's washed feet and new sandals. Smiling like God on the seventh day, the father offered his son a fat filet mignon, cooked with just the right amount of pink in the middle. Dad watched him eat, his face shining on him and beaming grace to him. But before the boy could finish his last bite, his father was on his feet again, singing and begging the son, "Come and dance!"

The boy's brain could not comprehend the day. How, in a few hours, had he gone from dirty to dancing?

Have you ever heard that story? It might be the most famous tale Jesus ever told. "The parable of the prodigal son" is what some Christians call it. The gospel of Luke, one of the four biographies of Jesus in the Bible, records this story that has inspired a million sermons—the final part of Jesus' trilogy on the joy of finding something that (or someone who) was lost.

But do you know why Jesus told that story? Luke tells us, "Now the tax collectors and sinners were all gathering around to hear Jesus. But the Pharisees and the teachers of the law muttered, 'This man welcomes sinners and eats with them.' Then Jesus told them this parable ... " (15:1-3). Ah, the tax collectors and "sinners," the notoriously dirty people from around town. Who would welcome filthy folks like them? Who would break bread with the morally broken? Who in their right mind would dare to dine with the dirtiest sinners on God's green earth?

According to Jesus, God would. If God would come walking into town, he would find the dirtiest people and tell them a story about a dirty kid who ended up dancing. I write that with absolute certainty because two thousand years ago, Jesus, who claimed to be God in human flesh, did come walking into town and did that very thing, told that very story.

That is why I am so happy you are reading this book. Because pornography has made lots of us feel dirty. Men and women. Adults and children. Church-leading pastors and churchgoing people. Our hearts feel like that son's feet: covered in the moral slop that a good night's sleep can't quite wash off.

Like the young woman who couldn't sleep because of porn. The guilt and the shame kept her up, gnawing at her soul. Her email arrived in my inbox at 3:09 A.M., a desperate cry for help. The devil, who hours earlier excused her potential sin, now was accusing her for agreeing with him. He would not let her believe she was anything but dirty, instead of one of the daughters God delights in.

Or like the young man studying to be a pastor. Despite years and years of Christian education, he wasn't even sure if God loved him anymore. He wasn't sure if he could actually be forgiven after the countless times he had sinned in dirty ways. The young man had sung "Jesus Loves Me, This I Know" for decades of his life, except he didn't "know" it anymore. Theologically, he knew better, but his conscience couldn't be so easily convinced. He felt too dirty to be loved by a holy God.

Or like the quiet couple on my counseling couch. He is brave enough to confess a struggle he never mentioned during all those years of dating. I watch her expression as he tells her. She, by God's grace, is forgiving like her Father in heaven, but the pain is real. No doubt she will wonder what she did wrong, why he turned to other girls, how much weight she should lose, why she isn't enough to satisfy him, and a thousand other irrational questions that come when porn dirties the intimacy between a man and his wife.

Or like the every-Sunday church attender who whispers to me after my porn presentation, "It's been 30 years." I see the hopelessness in his eyes as he questions whether his addiction will last 30 more.

Or like the woman who struggles with masturbation and has no clue to whom she should confide her dirty secret. Her pastor? Her Bible study friends? Are women allowed to confess that? Is anyone?

Or like the mom who finds the search history her kid hasn't yet learned how to erase. Appalled at the dirty words her "innocent" baby has learned to type, she is paralyzed by the question, "But isn't she too young?"

Or like me. For too long, porn conquered me. Despite all the church services I attended, the passages I memorized, and the prayers I prayed, I felt as dirty as the son in Jesus' story. My online wild living, though tame by today's standards of porn, was enough to make me question the authenticity of my faith. Could God save a wretched repeat offender like me?

Stories like these are not the outliers of a depraved culture. Unfortunately, they are the norm. Statistically, porn affects every pew. If you haven't struggled with online pornography and masturbation, the odds are that someone in your pew at church has. Jesus-loving, God-fearing, church-attending people that you love struggle with porn. Read that last sentence again and again until you believe it (it's okay, I can wait). Your loved ones struggle. Most of them just haven't told you yet.

No matter who you are—a porn addict, a concerned father, a frustrated wife, a girl whose boyfriend just confessed, a girl who just confessed to her boyfriend, a pastor who wants to help, a pastor who needs help, whoever—I am honored that you picked up this book. Thank you for being courageous enough to explore this taboo topic. God's church needs more people like you, people who care enough to reach out for help or to reach out to help others.

I'm not sure how your brain works, but my type-A wiring loves organization. I love knowing where we are going and when. So here are my four goals for our time together in the pages ahead:

First, I want to convince you that porn is bad. Really bad. Evil. Wicked. Dirty. Deadly. I want to show you that porn wants to kill nearly everything you love, proving there is no such thing as a consequence-free click.

Second, I want to show you that Jesus is good. Really good. Thrilling. Gracious. Forgiving. Unbelievably delighted in you. I want to prove that the Bible was written, in large part, about sexual sinners and for sexual sinners. I want you to dance as you feel the infectious beat of God's eternity-shaking grace.

Third, I want to compel you to make porn a public matter. Open. Honest. Vulnerable. Communal. Discussable. (This might be the point where you stop reading and tell yourself that another prayer might be all you need to fix a porn addiction. . . .) I want to use Scripture, my own story, and my experience in leading an anti-pornography ministry to show you that confessing to other people, and not just God, is one of the most powerful ways to conquer porn.

Finally, I want to give you a practical plan to go to war against porn. Doable. Workable. Clear. Effective. I want to share the tips that help God's kids stay out of the cesspools of porn. Some of those tips will challenge you, but all of them can help you overcome the sin that Jesus conquered on the cross.

So if you're ready for the journey, let's get you and those you love from dirty to dancing!

# 1

CHAPTER

# ⅅⅈℝⓉⓎ Looks

As I stand in the gas station mini-mart, I can't help but notice the marketing. My running partner, Nate, made it into the bathroom first, so I decide to stretch my quads and lust after the gas station donuts while I wait.[1] But then I notice the three letters wrapped around the stand-up cooler—XXX. Apparently, there is a new sports drink on the market, and the advertising gurus thought of this attention-getting name. After all, what is the first thing that comes to your mind when you think of electrolytes? Porn, right? Okay, maybe not . . .

But what gets my attention more than the branding is the tagline. It reads, "Because a little XXX never hurt anyone." Oh, really?

In a way, I wish that were true. I wish my past porn habits never hurt my wife. I wish I never had to hear the "I'll never be pretty enough" line from another brokenhearted wife from our church who just found out about her husband's problem. I wish I never met the kids who started looking in grade school and couldn't stop looking as their rewired brains craved more and more. I wish no one I knew ever went to jail because legal porn couldn't satisfy them anymore. I wish sexting wasn't an issue at my church, driven by the sex-pectations of teenagers raised

---

[1] *Lust,* according to my online dictionary, is "a passionate desire for something," which accurately describes the way I feel about donuts.

1

on porn. I wish porn never ended a man's ministry and left his church confused and his community shaking their heads. I wish the clever marketers were right. I wish a little porn never hurt anyone.

But they are not right. They are as far from right as left itself. Porn hurts everyone. Porn kills. Porn dirties the white-robed blessings our Father longs to give to his children.

This chapter is going to sting a bit, but I need you to read it. I need you to know what happens every time you click. I need you to know what will happen if you don't do something to protect your kids from their first click. I need you to know what we will lose if porn wins. Only then will we have the passion to go to war against porn.

## Porn Dirties _____.

**Porn dirties minds.** Smartphones scare me. Have you noticed in recent years how strong our thumbs are getting and how pathetic our eye contact has become? Our phones have us on a digital leash, demanding our attention and refusing to be ignored for more than a few minutes.

Why is that? What "changed" our minds? Answer: chemicals. God wired our brain with powerful chemicals, which, if not cautiously used, will turn us into itching, sweating, craving, gotta-get-a-hit addicts. When it comes to internet-connected devices, the unending variety and constant stimulation is a 24/7 opportunity to release more pleasure-inducing chemicals into our brains.

Which makes porn the perfect drug. The sexually exciting, potentially dangerous, and unending variety of porn releases ungodly amounts of dopamine (the pleasure chemical) into our brains. Combine porn with masturbation and, neurologists will tell you, the brain experiences dopamine levels similar to users

2

of crack cocaine. The brain screams, "Woohoo! That felt incredible! Let's do that again! Listen up, synapses! Shout, 'More of that!' on the count of three." Users start to crave that "high" like any addict with needle marks in her arms. And saying no becomes a complicated struggle, a detox that requires massive willpower and the selfless help of God, family, and friends.

Add the chemical oxytocin to the mix. Oxytocin is nicknamed the "cuddle hormone," the same chemical which floods the minds of mothers as they breast-feed, lovers after a night of intimacy, and porn users after another hit. Ever wonder why the big stud in the action movies gets all sappy and poetic after sleeping with the leading lady? Oxytocin! The mind is cuddling with—holding on to—the person who caused the dopamine rush. Or the pixels. Unable to tell the difference, the brain craves porn more and more with every click. It pushes our bodies to find the source of that intense pleasure we felt two nights ago. What might not cross the mind of the others in the business meeting now crosses yours. Oxytocin made it that way.

Then mix in the chemical epinephrine. Epinephrine, among other things, burns images into our minds like pictures saved on a hard drive. Our bodies want to remember vividly what caused that dopamine/oxytocin rush, so they take "snapshots" of those moments.

A podcast host in her late 20s recently recounted her experience as a six-year-old in a convenience store, recalling details of the first porn she ever held in her hands. A seminary professor once told me about the day when someone from the community pranked him, planting a dirty magazine in his mailbox. "Mike," he said (in his deep, professorial voice), "I can still remember the picture."

That's epinephrine. Sadly, that means lust isn't waiting until you choose to Google something sexual or gawk at the cute runner in your neighborhood. No, your mind will automatically supply the images, begging you, like a kid in the toy aisle,

"Can we look at this again? Can we do this again? Can we feel what we felt the other day?"

Get the point? Porn dirties your mind. It rewires your brain so that fleeing from sexual immorality means running into a fierce headwind, feeling like there's a magnet in your mind pulling you back into porn. Saying "No!" gets harder with every click. The compulsive behavior is so intense that even non-Christian sources are warning us about the "perfect drug" called porn. When the world agrees with the church, you know something evil is at work. . . .

I need you to remember all of this brain stuff if someone you love is struggling with porn. I know their porn use hurts you. You want your son, your wife, your boyfriend to just quit cold turkey. You want the tears you shed to be enough for them to shut off porn forever like a light switch. You want them to take their sin seriously and to love you not with apologies but with actions. I get it. And I agree with you. God does too. Jesus' goal is exactly that—for them to never look at porn again.

But a dirty mind cannot be cleaned up with a quick swipe of an emotional conversation. Their brain needs to be rewired, retaught, reprogrammed. They need to go through a detox of sorts, one that will require God's love and your patience. Not only is their sinful nature constantly craving more porn, their addicted brains are too. So pray passionately for the Holy Spirit to help you "be patient, bearing with one another in love" (Ephesians 4:2). They can change, but it will not be easy. They will need your help, your grace, and not more guilt.

On the other hand, if you yourself are struggling, take heart! The same brain you trained to crave porn can be retrained. Your old brain can learn new tricks. Neurologists call this neuroplasticity, meaning our brains are like moldable plastic, not unchangeable stone. Rewiring your brain will be agonizing at first—you will jitter like a drug addict in rehab—but week by week, God will renew and rewire your mind. Every day that you reject and resist porn is a day your brain gets better. Many former addicts notice a massive change after the 90-day threshold, when saying no to porn becomes a simple habit instead of a grueling struggle. I pray that one day you will look back and wonder, "Why was porn so hard to resist?"

True, porn dirties your mind. But God is able to clean it up.

**Porn dirties kids.** For years, I have promised parents that I would write a book entitled *Judgment Day Parenting*. The premise? You pray every day for Jesus to return before your daughter hits puberty![2] As a dad with two daughters whom I adore, I am more terrified than a cat at a dog park of the days when they grow up.

Which is why I should not have read the book *American Girls*. Author Nancy Jo Sales interviewed hundreds of teenage girls in America, chronicling their experiences in our digital age. *Mortified* would be too weak of a word to describe how I felt as I read Sales' findings, especially with porn. Porn is reaching and teaching the little girls that we love so much.

Combine fifth graders with the internet in their pockets, naive parents who are delaying the "talk" until high school, and curious classmates who are willing to Google anything, and—voila!—porn is the newest sex education class. Porn teaches third graders what sex "should" look like, namely, aggressive, easy, simple, demeaning. Porn teaches sixth graders how real "men" are supposed to act in bed, namely, like studs who can drive a woman wild with a single, sexy look. Porn teaches freshmen girls what boys want, namely, 24/7 sex and little else.

As a result, porn dirties our kids. John Chirban of Harvard Medical School laments, "With porn, you're not looking at the meaning and value of a whole human being. Girls take away from it the message that their most worthy attribute is their

---

2 Few points in my presentations get as much applause, especially from dads with daughters.

sexual hotness" (Sales, 17). Watch porn and personality is optional. Character, dialogue, and plot are fast-forwardable. All that matters is explicit sex. And kids are taking notes.

No wonder middle school boys are bold enough to request a "sext" from a girl they just met. No wonder high school girls, excited about their first kiss, are finding boys who have seen a lot more than kissing. No wonder interaction with living, breathing human beings is complicated compared to the easy "dialogue" with a video that can be paused, fast-forwarded, and replayed on command.

Can I plead with you parents to be more afraid of porn than you are of the awkward start to sexual conversations? We are grossly naive if we wait until prom night to talk about our children's sexuality. Studies show that the average age of exposure is around 11 years old (fifth grade). I first saw porn when I was still in the single digits. Unfortunately, today's first exposure is not the soft-core version that many of us had when we found a stash of magazines at a relative's house. That exposure is the hard-core video version that will unleash an explosion of chemicals in our babies' brains. So please, parents, protect your children. The world will preach one thousand toxic sermons to your children about porn. God is calling you to preach a few sermons too.

But there's an even more disturbing thought when it comes to children and porn—we are providing it. I am not suggesting that you encourage your kids to Google explicit content. But, in a roundabout way, you do that very thing if you look at porn. No, you might not get caught. No, it might be perfectly legal. No, you might only look every few weeks. But every time we click on porn, porn cashes the check. More clicks, more traffic, more ads, more money, more porn. Every click buys another bullet the porn industry will aim at my daughters, your nephews, and the children at your church. Many Christians think they can hide porn from their kids with locked doors and passwords, but as long as those kids use the same internet, our porn use is anything but hidden.

Those of us who have looked at porn cannot judgmentally wave a "Christian" finger at the immoral culture we live in or shake our heads at the stats of teenage pregnancy, unwed mothers, and social programs. We, in part, caused that. We set those kids up to fail when we promoted porn. We might have erased our search history, but we couldn't erase the consequences of our clicks.

Porn kills kids. Porn dirties their minds, their bodies, and their futures. Jesus warned, "If anyone causes one of these little ones—those who believe in me—to stumble, it would be better for them to have a large millstone hung around their neck and to be drowned in the depths of the sea" (Matthew 18:6). You don't have to search the dark corners of the web for child porn to find porn that dirties kids.

**Porn dirties marriages.** When my wife was first pregnant, we read a book called *What to Expect When You're Expecting.*[3] The premise of the title is that you need to know what to expect when a baby is on the way. Expect that little angel to act like an angel and you will have some hellish first nights! But expect your little bundle of joy to poop up his back, pee in your face, and vomit on your new sweater, and you'll avoid the shock of disappointment. It's amazing that some of us had a second kid, isn't it?

Expectations are everything. And nothing ruins our sexual expectations quite like porn. Porn, in case you haven't heard, is fake. There are cameras, makeup, scripts, lights, and a gaffer (the chief electrician in a motion picture—I Googled that). There are directors who shout "Cut!" and actresses who need a bathroom break and writers who are strategically thinking

---

3  Okay, she read it while I ate a tub of ice cream to satisfy my spousal sympathy cravings.

about viewers' preferences and perversions. Porn is not nonfiction. Porn is not real life. Porn is not what marriage is like.

In marriage, sex is great. Sometimes. And sometimes you shrug and smile, "Well . . . that just happened." In marriage, sex is frequent. Sometimes. And sometimes you are too busy or too overwhelmed or too sick for sex. In marriage, sex is spontaneous. Sometimes. And sometimes it's more like, "I have to finish these emails and pack the kids' lunches and vacuum, but if I get that done by 9:15, maybe we could squeeze in something quick." In marriage, husbands get headaches[4] and wives get menstrual cramps and couples get into arguments that make intimacy the last thing on their minds.

But in the world of porn, reality isn't good for business. Porn has to be passionate and explosive and shocking and loud to be profitable. If that's what we expect in marriage, we are setting ourselves up to be mad at our lover for so-so sex. Most porn has guys who are game for anything. If that's what we expect in marriage, we are going to pressure our lover into things he is not comfortable with. Most porn has girls who really mean yes when they say no. If that's what we expect in marriage, we are going to violate the sacred bond of God (and possibly even assault the one we married). Most porn has girls who are constantly craving it. If that's what we expect in marriage, we are going to pout when we wonder what's "wrong" with our lover. Porn exceeds realistic expectations. And expectations in marriage are everything.[5]

Ironically, porn often also changes the expectations of the spouse who doesn't watch it. Even if a porn user never said, "I wish you were like the women I watch in porn," that is still communicated. I don't need to think long to recall a half-dozen

---

4 Actually, I have never met a man who turned down sex due to a headache. For the majority of men, sex is like aspirin.

5 Technically, Jesus is everything, but anyone who has squabbled over the best way to load the dishwasher knows what I am saying.

stories of crying wives: "I'm not pretty enough. He must want me to look like those girls." And the husbands always say the same thing: "No, honey. It's not like that. I don't expect that. You are pretty. I do love you." But few wives believe it. Porn has forced them to expect that they will never be pretty enough, never be skinny enough, never be sexy enough. They will never be enough (and nothing fuels great intimacy like feeling totally inadequate . . . ).

This is one of the parts of my porn story that I wish I could erase. I was always attracted to my wife. I never thought less of her beauty because of my struggle with porn. But our early conversations about intimacy were filled with an unspoken assumption—porn changed the expectations. Those conversations were anything but the exciting exploration that God gives to a man and his bride in the long journey called marriage. Of the many things I wish I could change about my choices as a husband, this is at the top of my list. By God's grace, we have rebuilt what my porn use damaged, but it took a lot of hard conversations, some professional counseling, and an intense commitment to pursue her heart instead of breaking her heart with another click.

If you are married (or one day might be), refuse to let porn dirty your expectations. Refuse to let the lie of porn dirty your marriage.

**Porn dirties churches.** I had been trying to connect Pedro and Maria (names changed) to the gospel of Jesus for a long time. I met Pedro playing soccer, and one spiritual conversation turned into another. God opened a door of opportunity, and I baptized their daughter. Then they joined a Bible class to get familiar with Jesus' teachings. We immersed ourselves in God's grace and mercy and the work of Jesus on the cross. Everything was going great.

But things came to a screeching halt when we got to the lesson about the church and the importance of making a commitment to a local congregation. We studied God's desire for each of his kids to live in a Christian community, getting blessings and giving blessings to one another. Let us not give up meeting together. Let us encourage one another. Let us confess our sins to one another. Let us be kind and compassionate to one another. But the "let us" passages were met with scowls instead of smiles.

Pedro and Maria shared stories of the church they grew up in, where sex scandals with religious leaders were very public and all too common. "The church is filled with hypocrites," Maria insisted. "Why go if those people are worse than us anyway?"

Ouch. I tried to help Maria see the rest of the story. Not every church is like that. We do take sin seriously. We are all sinners. We need a church community to grow as God intended. Etc. Etc. But my words fell on deaf ears. The sexual sins of others had dirtied their view of the church. And they never came back.

Porn does that. In too many ways, porn dirties the church's external witness and its internal strength. Consider a few examples:

Pastor John hides his decade-long struggle with pornography, begging God to change his ways. He prays, then fails. Prays, then fails again. Prays, then fails some more. The problem, of course, is not his persistent prayers, but his unwillingness to embrace one of God's answers to prayer—honest Christian community. Instead, John's brain starts to get bored. The swimsuits don't fire his dopamine like they used to. So he searches for edgier porn and investigates on church-owned devices. Then, the unthinkable. His laptop crashes, and the church brings in the tech professionals to fix it. Guess what they find? Yup. When the news reaches the church elders and the rest of the staff, John's ministry is at risk, and his reputation is ruined.

Rachel is a small-group Bible study staple. Her biblical knowledge and ability to explain deep theology in simple terms is a blessing to everyone who attends. But when it comes time to talk about life, to confess sins and forgive one another in Jesus' name, Rachel smiles, "I'm . . . fine." But she's not fine. She has relapsed into a nasty habit of masturbation, often triggered by the ads on her favorite social media sites. But she hides that truth. She keeps it shallow. "Pray for my patience," she confesses to the other women, avoiding a request for the real prayers she needs. Following Rachel's lead, everyone in the room plays it safe, keeping one another an arm's distance from their actual struggles.

Greg used to be a rock star missionary. Blessed with a disarming smile and an ease in conversation, he would invest energy in every waitress, bank teller, and bartender he met. Spurred on by his love for their eternities, Greg would let his light shine and pray for the Holy Spirit to open the door to take conversations into spiritual waters. But then Greg got into porn. Porn dirtied his mind and corrupted his thoughts. Was it the dark and sinful part of his heart? The epinephrine? Both? Inappropriate ideas would flash into his mind at the most inappropriate times. He started to look at women differently. Not as souls to reach but as bodies to touch. Greg reversed Paul's claim, "From now on we regard no one from a worldly point of view" (2 Corinthians 5:16). Greg's view was definitely worldly. Now he imagined what good nights these girls could give him, not what good news he could give them.

I could go on. In the very place where God desires honesty, selflessness, and grace, porn inserts lies, selfishness, and guilt. Porn dirties ministries and ministers. Porn dirties fellowship and community. Porn dirties churches.

**Porn dirties souls.** As a young boy, I never imagined I would question my salvation. After all, I grew up in a church culture that specialized in emphasizing the saving work of Jesus Christ in every sermon, every service, and every Bible study. We took sin seriously, but we took grace seriously-er. (I'm making up words to show you how serious we were!) I knew from my seventh grade Bible class that the dos and don'ts of the Bible show us our sins and the good news about Jesus shows us our Savior. When the law has struck you, humbled you, and terrified you, run to the gospel! Run to Jesus! Run to grace and mercy and peace at the cross!

That beautiful teaching was my weekly meal every Sunday. But as I lay there in bed, I somehow forgot all of it. No, I hadn't drifted from church. I went every Sunday (even as a teenager when Mom couldn't make it). I prayed every day (and not just token dinner prayers sped through like an auctioneer). I read my Bible every single day (even keeping a notebook to check the boxes of the chapters I read). But despite my devotion to the spiritual disciplines, my soul was a mess.

"Am I really a Christian? Christians are repentant; they are sorry for their sins. Am I sorry? Sorry enough? I say I'm sorry, but why did I go back to porn? Why did I do that again? Why don't I just stop if I say I love God so much?" I would lie in bed, staring at the ceiling. In fact, my failures happened so often that I actually had a CD with all of my favorite "repentance songs." When Jars of Clay would sing, "I am the only one to blame for this/Somehow it all ends up the same," I would cry (again) and confess (again) and wonder if God could forgive me (again). Porn had dirtied my soul.

As I reflect on those dark years, my most vivid memory is of my carpeted stairs. A few years later, after getting married, I had snuck off downstairs to the computer to indulge in porn after my wife fell asleep. Trudging up the carpeted stairs, I immediately felt the guilt. "Why did I do that? I am so sorry, God." I crawled quietly back into bed, embarrassed and weak. For ten minutes, I stared at the wall in the darkness, feeling hollow and empty. But moments later, a thought welled up in my heart, "I could do that again." And, I am ashamed even to type this, I got out of bed. Went back downstairs. Logged on the computer. Went back to the same sites. Erased the search history again. And went back up the carpeted stairs.

How could I claim to love God? How could I claim that my tears of repentance had anything to do with repentance? I know the answer to those questions now—the flesh is way worse than we imagine. Unteachable. Irreversibly hostile to obedience. But in the moment, the frequency of my sin dirtied my soul beyond the belief that I was actually saved. While sin is eternally serious and can lead us to reject the Holy Spirit (1 Thessalonians 4:8), I had forgotten the beautiful truth that where sin increases, grace increases all the more (Romans 5:20).

In 1 Corinthians chapter 6, Paul says something that, at first, does not sound theologically correct. Paul claims that all sin is not the same. Listen to his words: "All other sins a person commits are outside the body, but whoever sins sexually, sins against their own body" (6:18). All other sins . . . but sexual sins? What does that mean? I can think of a ton of sins that happen with my body—my fists can punch, my ears can lean toward gossip, my feet can trip someone in soccer. Other sins like drunkenness or drug use can hijack the chemicals in my brain too. So what is so unique about sexual sins that they deserve their own category?

I could be completely wrong here, but I suspect sexual sin has a uniquely dirtying effect on our emotional health (not to mention its effect on our relationships, souls, etc.). The guilt, shame, and secrecy of sexual sins have a way of weighing us down and ruining not just our souls but also the bodies that are connected to them. Think of the young woman moping around all morning after an evening tryst with porn. Think of the nervous pressure the college-aged Christian feels as he decides whether or not to lie to his accountability partner about his past week. Think of how a newly married woman's entire day is plagued by the burden of telling her unsuspecting husband what happened.

Do you agree? I sense there is something uniquely shameful about porn. In healthy church communities, we can confess impatience with a boss or anger with backed-up traffic or a struggle to forgive an abusive ex-boyfriend. But porn is a different story, even when the church is solidly committed to the free forgiveness of Jesus. Confess you drank too much, and you will see the knowing smirks and nodding heads. But confess you masturbate too much, and few people will join you in your confession, even if their consciences are nodding in agreement. Our souls feel different with sexual sin. Like Adam and Eve, we are tempted to flee from the light and cover up our habits with the fig leaves of our fabricated stories (Genesis 3:7).

Thus, porn doesn't just dirty our lives for a few minutes after a fall. It can ruin hours, days, even weeks as our consciences accuse us of being too dirty to step out into the light of confession, community, and grace. Porn dirties our souls.

**Porn dirties everything.** I wish the list of porn's victims ended there. Depressingly, it does not. Porn dirties our world, as the easy money from the love of porn translates into the horrors of the sex trafficking industry. Porn dirties our purpose, as we waste hours every month surfing for just the right video instead of serving, praying, and loving others. Porn dirties our future relationships, as we train our brains for digital cheating. Porn dirties . . . well, you get the point.

I told you this was going to sting. When God opens your eyes to see that our clicks are dirtying bodies and souls, marriages and ministries, nephews and nieces, daughters and sons, consciences and communities; when we first realize that we have participated in sex trafficking, funding one of the most horrific industries on the planet; when it dawns on us that those clicks put Christ on his cross . . . sin stings. And that's what porn is.

Sin. God hates it because he hates what it does to those he loves. You included. Your heavenly Father wants you to know that there is no such thing as a clean click.

# Pornolatry

So given all the dirty effects of porn, why do so many Christians indulge so often? That is a question Bruno Mars can help us answer.

You may know Bruno Mars as a ubiquitous pop star who took over the radio for a few years. His lyrics are probably not appropriate for the kindergarten concert,[6] but they are helpful in understanding porn's allure. In his smash hit "Locked Out of Heaven," Mars sings, "Never had much faith in love or miracles/Never wanna put my heart on the line/But swimming in your water is something spiritual/I'm born again every time you spend the night/Cause your sex takes me to paradise."[7]

Did you notice what Mr. Mars is saying? Having sex is like being in paradise, like enjoying the joys of heaven itself. And, as the song goes on to say, not having sex is like being "locked out of heaven."

Mars has a point. Sex is a lot like heaven. Sex, when done as God intended, is intimate, exciting, safe, pleasurable, anticipatory, and a whole lot of fun. Although the highest pleasures of sex are momentary, they are some of the most intense experiences that human beings can have in this life.

According to the Bible, those experiences are meant to get us really, really, really excited about heaven. Seriously. The angels in heaven sing, "The whole earth is full of [God's] glory," and

---

[6] My friend once sent me a video of some 80-year-olds in choir robes singing hip-hop hits and I nearly died laughing, so maybe the kindergarten idea is worth thinking about. . . .

[7] For the record, I left out a number of "uhs!" and "oh yeah, yeahs!"

the apostle Paul insisted that God's divine nature is "clearly seen, being understood from what has been made" (Isaiah 6:3; Romans 1:20). God's nature, that is, what God is like, is experienced right here in this life. This life gives us a tiny taste, a bite-sized appetizer, of the feast in heaven. All the laughter and comfort and delights and wonders and joys and, yes, pleasures of this life are meant to get us excited about basking in the presence of the glory of God!

So Mars was almost right. Sex gives us a glimpse of paradise. To be so exposed and yet accepted by another human being, the definition of true intimacy, is a glimpse of being totally known by God and yet absolutely accepted by him. To be excited about what is to come is a glimpse of the excitement we will feel about our unending and never-boring future with God. To be consumed by a euphoric feeling in sex is a glimpse of the non-sexual euphoria we will feel when we see the face of God.

No wonder King David declared, "You will fill me with joy in your presence, with eternal pleasures at your right hand" (Psalm 16:11). Eternal pleasures! Pleasures, even better than earth's highest pleasures, last eternally when you are in the very presence of God. If that doesn't get you amped up about eternity, I am not quite sure what will!

But did you notice what else Mars crooned? "Never had much faith in love or miracles/Never wanna put my heart on the line." Experience taught him that love is a dangerous thing. When you love someone, you put your heart on the line. Pursue an actual person and she might reject you, challenge you, expose your selfish flaws. A boyfriend might leave you, forsake you, even replace you. A billion breakup songs prove that Mars is not alone.

This is why porn picks up so many Christian partners. Do you want the thrill, the anticipation, the pleasure, without the potential of rejection? Do you want a taste of heaven without the pressure of asking someone out and without the possibility of a text he reads but doesn't return? Then porn is calling, "Call upon me in the day of trouble. I will deliver you!" Porn seems like the perfect partner. Let me explain a few reasons why.

First, porn is always there for you. In the real world, it might take forever to find someone who is personally and sexually interested in you. In the porn world, you can find a thousand girls who will give you "the look" as quickly as you can type "porn" and hit enter. In the real world, you can get rejected, dumped, and divorced. In the porn world, the guys are always interested in you. Porn taps into our human need to be accepted, included, and wanted.

Second, porn leverages our love of excitement. In the real world, we travel to the Grand Canyon and Mexican beaches to see something new and different and exciting. In the porn world, there is always something new and different and exciting. New actors and actresses. New body shapes and sizes. New races. New everything. In the real world, vacations take time and money, two resources we often lack. In the porn world, most content is free and immediately accessible. Our brains crave variety, and porn provides an open buffet of endless variety whenever you want.

Third, porn promises us escape from our lives. In the real world, we worry about car loans, GPAs, second interviews, grouchy neighbors, kids who won't nap, hardheaded coworkers, chores that need to be done (and then redone days later), and so much more. In the porn world, there is an escape from worry. Our brains get laser-focused on naked bodies, escaping from the challenges of our actual lives. Even if it's just for a few minutes, porn is an all-inclusive vacation from life.

Fourth, porn offers us power. In the real world, we sometimes feel weak. We can't get what we want in relationships. People hurt us and belittle us. In the porn world, we can get back at them. Did your wife reject your not-so-subtle offer to have sex? You can regain power and punish her with porn. Did

17

the boys at school ignore you all week long? You can find porn that humiliates men and makes you feel like you are in control. With porn, *we* click, *we* replay, *we* control the action. Porn makes us powerful.

Locked out of paradise? Maybe when an actual person denies you sex but never in the world of porn. The men and women of porn never lock the door. In fact, they installed an automatic door to make it easy for you to enter their world.

This is what I call *pornolatry*—the idolatry of porn. The replacing of our cravings for God with his knockoff counterparts. Porn is the Rolex on sale for $39.99 at the tourist stop in Mexico City. Porn is the Burberry purse you can buy for $20 on the streets of Tokyo. Porn is getting what you want at a price you can afford. At least that is what porn claims . . .

I have a statue of a naked woman in my office. She has small breasts, but lots of them. Twenty-three actually.[8] The statue is named Artemis. Artemis was the many-breasted fertility goddess of the ancient Greeks. The temple of her statue in Ephesus was one of the seven wonders of the ancient world. I bought a mini version of the statue when I visited Ephesus years ago, which now sits on my shelf. Actually, I first heard about Artemis from a college professor who said that some former students had dressed up as Artemis using a complex arrangement of water balloons. If that didn't win the best Halloween costume, something is wrong with the world . . .[9]

I have to laugh when I see that little statue. The Greeks seemed like intelligent people, so how in the world did they worship a big statue of a woman with two dozen breasts? Seems crazy, right? Well, maybe not. Maybe they had this craving for healthy

8 I just counted them and was really glad that no one walked by my office window.

9 If you were raised conservative Lutheran, like I was, Halloween is the world's version of All Saints Day, when you might have dressed up as one of the heroes of the Reformation.

families and fertility. Maybe they were aching to get pregnant and hold a son in their arms. Maybe they wanted something good and simply turned to the wrong place to get it.

Sounds like porn, doesn't it? We have this craving to be loved, known, desired, and included. We ache for excitement and pleasure and an escape from our worries. Maybe we just want something good and turn to a perverted place to get it.

We might call it Satan's Dirty Trick. The devil tricks us by trying to satisfy our cravings for God with an ineffective alternative. Like a cold beer or a swallow of salt water, porn seems to quench our thirst . . . but then it leaves us more parched than ever. When we finally close the browser, our problems are still there. Actually, they are bigger than before, since we have added shame, secrets, wasted time, and the dirtying effects of porn to our mess. Just like a drug, porn worked for a while. But the "while" was way shorter than promised. God cannot be replaced, no matter how clever the marketing.

The previous pastor at my church had a helpful refrain: STP=LTP. Short Term Pleasure=Long Term Pain. That's Satan's dirty trick. He pushes us toward porn, partnering with our own sinful flesh and the money-hungry systems of the world, promising us a glimpse of heaven. But when the dopamine dies down, we plunge back into the long-term pain of sin, feeling far from God, far from love, locked out of paradise.

So will you let me speak boldly enough to expose the Father of Lies' lies? Will you let me magnify the fine print and explain what our 21st-century version of Artemis likes to leave out? As we continue our journey to see how dirty and destructive porn is, here are ten things porn won't tell you. We have already covered a few of them briefly, but some things are worth hearing a second time.

**10. I WON'T SATISFY YOU (FOR LONG).** When assaulted with temptation, porn seems like a satisfying answer. Porn is the athlete's foot of the mind, which screams to be scratched. But if you scratch, the itch intensifies. Porn satisfies for seconds, then leaves us with long-term wreckage. But porn never told you that.

**9. I WANT YOUR MONEY, NOT YOU.** One of the goals of porn producers is to make you feel sexy. After all, if this uber-sexy actress is looking at "you" that way, you must be desirable. But that's a lie. The producers don't know you or care one bit about your body, soul, faith, or family. All they know is that your "anonymous" click is worth money. Greed, not sexual expression, fuels this industry. We may not call porn "prostitution," yet exchanging sex for money sounds like an accurate definition. But porn never told you that.

**8. I WILL GET DARK—FAST.** No drug addict imagines herself with festering sores on her face, trembling hands, and the inability to hold a rational conversation for more than 17 seconds. But that's where the path of drug addiction leads. Likewise, no one dabbling with still images of half-naked men imagines where this could lead. Once the drug of "normal" porn fails to arouse like it used to, where will you go? Hard-core porn? Violent porn? Gay porn? Transgender porn? Child porn? Most would be appalled at the suggestion, but porn is a drug, and what satisfies today will not satisfy tomorrow. The law of diminishing returns is true with our sexuality too. Today's porn will only make it tempting to say yes to tomorrow's darkness, a shade of grey you never imagined you would enjoy. But porn never told you that.

**7. I WILL EXTORT YOU.** Once porn has hijacked your brain, it won't let you go. Porn has an ability to fill you with shame, a shame so great that you won't feel able to confess your addiction to anyone else. While you will almost surely need the help of your church, your friends, and your family, porn will convince you that you could never admit the things you've seen and done. Thus, porn extorts you, continuing to take your clicks, downloads, and dollars and leaving you with fear, shame, and regret. But porn never told you that.

**6. I MIGHT COST YOU YOUR CAREER.** You don't have to be in full-time ministry to fear the workplace consequences of porn. Computers remember. They remember your digital past. And computers crash. They need to be fixed by people who are experts in retrieving the past. What happens when the boss finds out the searches done on company time? What happens when your coworkers hear the rumors about what I.T. found on your computer? But porn never told you that.

**5. SHE WAS RAPED.** While not all porn stars have been violated sexually, many have. They learned to equate sex with love from the molestation, rape, and sexual abuse of their past. They learned to find their worth in their ability to please another man. God's heart breaks over the sins committed against them and desires to rescue them from the messages imposed on them by their abusers. If we can get aroused after knowing that, there is something deeply wrong with our hearts. But porn never told you that.

**4. I MIGHT SNATCH AWAY YOUR FRIEND'S SOUL.** In increasing numbers, Americans label Christians as "hypocritical." While we may contend with their definition (since being a Christian implies confessing you are so messed up that you couldn't save yourself), we also understand the importance of living a godly life. Church scandals and sexual sins among the people in the pews shove curious unbelievers away from the Word of God. "What's the point," many wonder, "if they do the same stuff I do?

At least I get to sleep in on Sundays." Porn might cost your church a chance to reach your community with the message of forgiveness. But porn never told you that.

**3. I WILL STALK YOU.** The human brain is an incredible creation of God. Like a computer hard drive, it can store images and memories for years, if not more. God gave us the ability to remember and memorize his Word, to recall stories of his forgiveness, and to bring back Grandma's smile, even years after her passing. But porn uses that good gift for evil purposes. Once an explicit image is viewed, it doesn't erase with the internet history. The brain stores it. And, like a haunted hard drive out to get you, that image will be a mental pop-up ad that will stalk you for months, if not years. Just take a peek today and porn will give you peeks for thousands of days to come. But porn never told you that.

**2. GOD SEES.** Most porn is viewed in private. Behind the monitor at work. On a phone in the bathroom. On the office laptop. If our conscience is still functioning, we recognize the shame of it all and desire to hide it. But God still sees. God sees the sin we commit behind closed doors. Your mom or girlfriend or husband may never find out. You may have learned how to hide the magazine, erase the internet history, or bury the video file in some obscure folder. However, the holy God of heaven and earth sees. But porn never told you that.

**1. YOUR SOUL COULD GET USED TO ME.** If you are repentant (you feel sorrow for this evil and believe Jesus forgives it) for your sexual sin today, thank God. It is true that God is infinitely merciful, and he will forgive a lifetime of porn that we confess to him, nailed to the cross of Jesus. But will you be repentant tomorrow? The apostle Paul warned the Christians at Ephesus, a city filled with

Artemis-related porn, about the domino effect of "hardening your hearts" to sexual sin. Once you get used to porn and aren't real about the wreckage, you won't confess it as quickly or sorrowfully. Soon, your thinking about porn will change and you might justify it by saying, "My spouse isn't interested," or, "I just need a quick release." Before you realize it, you will lose "all sensitivity" to this sin, as Paul warns. If you live in this sin with no remorse or regret, you could lose your soul (Ephesians 4:17-19). But porn never told you that.

I know, this has been brutal, but I also know that the enemy has convinced God's kids to excuse, rationalize, and minimize the evil of pornography. Sex is a brilliant invention of God, a glimpse of heaven. Porn is a pathetic knockoff of God's promises, a taste of hell. So trust your loving Father, porn is not a shortcut to what your heart craves. Porn is a highway to long-term pain. That is why God insists that porn is dirty.

Which explains the dirty scene of the cross. There is Jesus, the holy Son of God, whose soul was the original Mr. Clean, looking filthy. Their spit, his blood, the bugs, the nails, his bodily fluids, their insults. The cross is disgusting, as dirty as all the world's porn put together. But it was the only way to make dirty people clean. Jesus was the only way dirty people could end up dancing. . . .

# 2

# The DIRTY Can Dance

For a scrawny, 6' 2" Caucasian, I am a pretty good dancer. I spent an entire year training in my basement for a dance battle with a guy named Jakey G. No joke. Jakey G was rumored to be Appleton, Wisconsin's best dancer and we were both going to be at a wedding together, so our mutual hairstylist set up the battle. Being wired as a competitor, I trained hard. My incredible wife bought me some Adidas with the white stripe on the bottom to emphasize my moonwalking skills that I was learning from YouTube. I learned how to glide, wave, Harlem shake, and baby freeze. Compared to the average Midwestern, conservative, Lutheran pastor, I was killing it![10]

The wedding day arrived and I was nervous. I had never met Jakey G, but assumed he would roll in with a flat-brimmed hat and some fresh Adidas (and perhaps his own cardboard for breakdancing). And then someone said, "There's Jake!" I looked and saw a scrawny, 6' 2" Caucasian—my twin brother with a beard. Apparently, Jakey G barely knew about this dance battle, and my choreographed dance number did not turn out as expected.[11]

---

[10] Based on my observation, the average Midwestern, conservative, Lutheran pastor only knows the polka and, perhaps, the Electric Slide.

[11] Ironically, two people saw my breakdancing that night and decided to come to our church! God works in very mysterious ways. . . .

Do you like dancing? Lots of people don't. Two left feet and a fear of embarrassment keep lots of us off the dance floor. Yet there are times when we have to dance, when we jump and bounce and throw our hands in the air. You see this at sporting events when the joy of a last-second victory erupts through the stadium and guys who never would touch the dance floor jump around with the blasting music.

Dancing, in most cultures, is a sign of joy. We don't dance at funerals, but we do at weddings. Show off "the worm" in front of Grandma's casket and people will stare. Do the same move at a rocking reception and people will cheer.

My favorite phrase from Jesus' famous story of the Dirty Son is "When [the older brother] came near the house, he heard music and dancing" (Luke 15:25). The merciful father apparently hired a DJ and was telling the whole town about his joy. This isn't the only reference to dancing in the Bible. Moses' sister Miriam danced with her female friends after God's miraculous Red Sea rescue. Israel danced when Goliath fell and brave David came into town. David himself once danced so hard that his wife was embarrassed enough to die! All of these stories remind us that God's presence and grace is cause for dancing. "You turned my wailing into dancing; you removed my sackcloth and clothed me with joy" (Psalm 30:11).

Most people who struggle with porn don't feel like dancing. They feel dirty, like that kid with filthy feet and a long history of dirty deeds. But Jesus gives us a reason to dance, even if we have done dirty things.

## The Dirty to Dancing Half-Dozen

The Bible seems to be written for sexual sinners. While internet porn is a modern problem, God's explicit love for those who have viewed explicit images and done explicit things was evident even in ancient times. Journey with me through the Bible as we see men and women who danced despite their dirty choices.

**David:** Years after David killed Goliath, another giant killed David: lust. As the new king of Israel, David could have anything he wanted, so he decided to use his royal power to satisfy his sexual desire. He stole another man's wife, impregnated her, and killed her husband to cover his tracks. David, who was supposed to be a "man after [God's] own heart" (1 Samuel 13:14), was now a man after his own flesh. Nevertheless, God intervened in love and brought a message of repentance and forgiveness to David through the prophet Nathan. Reflecting on his sin and God's grace, David later wrote, "When I kept silent, my bones wasted away. . . . Then I acknowledged my sin . . . and you forgave the guilt of my sin" (Psalm 32:3,5). Lust, adultery, murder, and almost a year of hiding instead of confessing, yet God's grace was still great enough to forgive all the guilt David had incurred.

Like David, you may be hiding sexual sin. You may fear the repercussions of what you've done. While there may be earthly consequences to this sin, the spiritual consequences were absorbed by Jesus on the cross. The guilt, the shame, the sin, the punishment, the anger—everything that would affect us eternally—was paid in full by your Savior. Jesus forgave it and rose from the dead to make you new in the sight of God. So confess to him freely, and know that his grace is sufficient for you! God is not ashamed to have real sinners as part of his family.

Last summer, the Novotny family had a reunion. At the end of the night, someone handed me a book of old records, newspaper clippings, and pictures. That's when I first met my great-grandpa. The Kewaunee paper ran the story—"Kewaunee man shoots himself with shotgun in barn". *Why have I never heard of this?* I thought. And then my cousin whispered to me when no one was around, "You've heard about so-and-so, right?" Um, no. She shared the story of the abuser in our family tree. *Why have I never heard of this?* I thought. But I knew the answer. We don't like to talk about those people. We bring up the bright lights, not the black sheep.

So why didn't Matthew do that? Matthew wrote the first biography of Jesus that we find in the Bible, but he begins in a surprising way. In order to get to the birth of Jesus in Matthew's gospel, you first have to go through the crooked branches in his family tree: guys like David, Jesus' infamous ancestor who lusted and stole for sexual pleasure. "This is the genealogy of Jesus the Messiah the son of David" (Matthew 1:1), and then a few lines later the genealogy specifically mentions that Jesus' ancestor David had taken "Uriah's wife." Why not edit those parts out? What point is Matthew trying to make? Here's the answer: Christ came from and for sinners. Christ came from all kinds of sinners. And Christ came for all kinds of sinners. So if you ever wonder if Christ came for someone like you, just read the list of the someones from whom Christ came.

**The Samaritan Woman:** The Samaritans were a sinful bunch. In Jesus' culture, to call someone a Samaritan was on par with calling them demon-possessed. So we would expect Jesus to keep his distance from people with such sordid reputations. But he didn't. He walked right into the heart of Samaria, right to a well where he knew an ostracized Samaritan woman would be. (Imagine how sinful she must have been to not fit in with the other Samaritans!) There, he spoke of a "living water" that he could give her, a water that would satisfy her in a way the revolving door to her bedroom never could. Shocked and sanctified, the woman ran to tell her Samaritan neighbors of the one who told her what no one else ever did. She was loved and forgiven by God. This is why, unlike his religious neighbors who avoided Samaria at all costs, Jesus insisted that he *"had to go through Samaria"* (John 4:4).

If you are looking for love, worth, acceptance, forgiveness, and satisfaction for your soul, look no further than Jesus. Jesus came into this world because God loved us so much. Our Savior might say, "I *had to* send that missionary to your city, into your school, into your family. I *had to* in order to reach out to you, the sexual sinner who assumed she was too dirty to dance with God."

Jesus gives us incalculable worth by making us part of God's family and heirs of all his spiritual blessings. Jesus' forgiveness makes us acceptable to God—no, more than that—it makes God's face shine on us whenever he looks in our direction. We see his smile of grace instead of his scowl of justice.

**The Corinthians:** Sexual sin was so prevalent in the ancient city of Corinth that a new Greek verb was invented—*Corinthiadzomai.* That meant to "act like a Corinthian," which meant "to be sexually immoral." When they invent a verb to describe your sexual sin, you know it's bad! Yet the apostle Paul preached the message of Jesus' life, death, and resurrection for even the Corinthians. He once wrote to them, "You were washed, you were sanctified, you were justified in the name of the Lord Jesus Christ and by the Spirit of our God" (1 Corinthians 6:11). Jesus' saving work made the Corinthians holy brothers in the faith, despite the label they had earned.

You too may have a label for yourself. Unclean. Sick. Twisted. Dirty. Depraved. Pathetic. Godless. Shameful. Corinthian. But your sin doesn't get the last word. Jesus came "to seek and to save the lost" (Luke 19:10), and if your label says "lost," that means Jesus came into this world for you. His blood washes away the ink on your nametag, and he himself writes a new name on you, a name that only he can give: Saint. Holy. Perfect. Blameless. Pure. Clean. Loved. Saved.

If you ever have the chance to visit Greece, make sure you stop by ancient Corinth. The ruins of an ancient courtroom sit below a towering mini-mountain called the Acrocorinth. In New Testament times, that hill was famous for sexuality. Perched above the city, in clear view of all the Corinthians, was the temple of Aphrodite, the goddess of pleasure. According to nonbiblical sources, one thousand priestess-prostitutes "served" in that temple, helping the citizens of Corinth and the sailors who passed through town to "worship" the goddess. No wonder they invented that verb . . .

If you stand down in that ancient courtroom, look up to that mountain. Think of the mountain of evidence of your sexual sin. Shudder at the thought of what the judgment would be if the judge took all the evidence into account. But then think of that beautiful promise that an ancient king named Hezekiah clung to. God, he confessed, "you have put all my sins behind your back" (Isaiah 38:17). Think of God, the judge, looking down at you, with the mountain of your sin behind his back. Not hanging above your head. Not clinging to your heart. But behind his back. You might see it, think about it, remember it, but not God. The judge just smiles down at you and Jesus and declares, "Not guilty!"

**Judah:** As they make their way through the soap-operalike stories of the book of Genesis—the very first book of the Bible— no readers would guess that Jesus would come from the line of Judah. Judah's family was famous for its dysfunction, but Judah took his family's drama to a whole new level. One day, Judah's daughter-in-law Tamar got pregnant while working as a prostitute. Judah, claiming to hate sexual sin, demanded her death. But what Judah failed to mention was that he himself had a thing for motel rentals by the hour. And, if his last prostitute hadn't been wearing a veil, Judah would have known she was . . . yup . . . his daughter-in-law. Yet despite that hypocrisy, centuries later Jesus chose to be known as the Lion of Judah.

Maybe you have been as hypocritical as Judah. Maybe you have judged others for their sexual promiscuity. Maybe you have vented about single moms and immoral entertainment. Maybe you have scolded your kids for their sexual sins. And maybe you were sexually sinning the entire time.

Despite the hypocrisy, Jesus chose to be known as your big brother. "Both the one who makes people holy and those who are made holy are of the same family. So Jesus is not ashamed to call them brothers and sisters" (Hebrews 2:11). Jesus is not ashamed to be related to hypocrites. Jesus is not ashamed to be close to you.

"Feel free to skip the boring parts of the Bible." That's what the pastor told us. I was visiting a church in my old town, taking notes from the back pew. The preacher definitely got my attention when he put the words "boring" and "Bible" into the same sentence. *This is God's Word!* I thought. *The Holy Spirit wrote this,* I thought. But do you know what else I thought? *He's kind of right.* Because the parts he was talking about were the names. The genealogies. The endless lists of names no one volunteers to read at Bible study. The family trees. And they are about as fun as reading the phonebook.

Remember what we learned before about Jesus' family tree? It is there not to bore us, but to thrill us. And not just because of David. Look who else shows up on this list—"This is the genealogy of Jesus the Messiah . . . Judah the father of Perez and Zerah, whose mother was Tamar . . . " (Matthew 1:1,3). There is something thrilling when you open the New Testament and see the name of a hypocritical, sexual sinner next to the name of our Savior. Because you know that Jesus bled and died even for people like us.

**Rahab:** A prostitute should, by definition, be excluded from a list of God's holy and faithful people. Rahab was such a woman, carrying out "the oldest profession on earth" around

1400 B.C. However, when God's people came to her city, she confessed her faith in a God of faithful love, a God filled with love for the unlovable.

You may have a past as twisted as Rahab's, but God is not letting that stop him. The apostle Paul says, "Where sin increased, grace increased all the more" (Romans 5:20). Your sexual sin may have been building up for years, even decades, but the broom of grace is bigger than the mess you have made. Even prostitutes and porn addicts are not too big of a mess to be made new in Christ.

Did you hear when Kanye West and Kim Kardashian had a second baby? Kanye, based on his song lyrics, is a wannabe god, a rapper unafraid to take the gavel from God himself. Kim, based on almost everything she posts, is a selfie-addicted stripper. And when those two had a baby, do you know what they named him? Saint. Saint West. Lots of people laughed at that name. Doesn't seem like the best choice . . .

But you know what's even more shocking than Saint West? Saint Me. Saint You. A "saint" in biblical terms is a holy person, which is what Jesus died to make us. Read once more about the identity-changing work of our Savior: "Both the one who makes people holy and those who are made holy are of the same family" (Hebrews 2:11).

**The Adulterous Woman:** When the self-righteous religious leaders caught a woman having sex outside of marriage, they dragged her to Jesus and demanded her death. Jesus replied with the now infamous line, "Let any one of you who is without sin be the first to throw a stone at her" (John 8:7). Convicted, all the accusers left, leaving this cheating woman alone with Jesus. The problem? Jesus, the Son of God, was without sin and there were plenty of stones lying around for him to pick up. So what did Jesus do? Jesus looked her in the eye and said, "Neither do I condemn you" (John 8:11).

That's the heart of Jesus towards you too. Although you are guilty as sin, his desire is not to condemn you but to forgive you. In fact, he has already forgiven you, cleansing you of your filth in the water of his mercy and dropping the charges against you through his death on the cross. Why would he not? Because Jesus made sure that your sin has nothing to do with you.

That kind of love makes me think of the Dead Sea. A few years back, I got to float in the Dead Sea. If you haven't heard, the Dead Sea is so thick with salt that human beings become buoyant. No floaties required! You jump in and bob at the surface as if there were an inflatable ring around your waist. A friend video recorded my first trip into the Dead Sea, where, if the footage is to be believed, I giggled like a seven-year-old girl.

What does that have to do with the joy of God's grace? Listen to the prophet Micah: "[God, you will] hurl all our iniquities into the depths of the sea" (Micah 7:19). Think about that. We float in the warm sun of God's love and our sins stay at the bottom of the sea! God sees us up here and hides our sins down there. God, as one Christian put it, drowns our sins and then posts a sign that says, "No fishing."

Have I given you enough proof? From lusters and liars to adulterers and cheaters, the Bible is filled with proof that dirty people can dance. Therefore, your sexual sin is not the exception to the blanket statements of God's love and forgiveness for the world.

## Doing vs. Dancing

I will admit that this chapter has not been very practical. We Christians love practical. Have you noticed that? One of the best ways to sell books or write blogs is to start with a number and follow it with a felt need. Five Steps to a Better Marriage.

Three Food Choices to Revolutionize Your Diet. Two New Ways to Pray. I am convinced that if you want to get more traffic on your website or social media platform, just pick any number and then attach a life-changing promise to it.[12]

Maybe this chapter has not felt step-y enough for you. "Mike, what do I do? I hate porn, so what steps do I need to take?" "Okay, Jesus loves us, but my spouse's porn is killing our relationship, so what do we do next?" To which I respond, "Simmer down now!"[13]

Steps are great. In fact, before this book is done, I am going to give you some concrete, practical steps to take as you and your loved ones battle for the joys of purity. But before we rush into our American pragmatism, let us not forget the power of the gospel of God's love for sexual sinners. Since we all love numbers, here are three reasons why we should not rush past the gospel.

## 1. THE GOSPEL PROMISES AN ETERNITY OF DANCING.

Imagine if porn's only consequence was eternal condemnation. Imagine if porn was consequence-free in this life. Imagine if porn was a wonderful way to improve your mood, self-esteem, relationships, family, and society. Imagine if porn was a free way to vacation from your problems and there was no porn hangover the next morning. Imagine if you did not have to hide your porn, but your parents and your pastor and your friends and your kids and your significant others were all ecstatic that you indulged every day.

But imagine if that all ended when you died. If you were too dirty to dance with God in heaven. If you were too filthy to fit in with the holy angels and the saints in glory. If you were too

---

[12] In full disclosure, Conquerors through Christ has "5 Steps to Reject Porn" on its website, but that is different because . . . um . . . never mind.

[13] Am I the only one who remembers that SNL skit with Garth Brooks? I give you permission to Google it before you continue reading.

impure to enjoy all God's presence had to offer. In other words, if you could gain the whole world through porn, but had to give up your soul, would it be worth it?

Absolutely not. Porn would be the ultimate STP=LTP. Even if the pleasure lasted one hundred years, it would still seem so short compared to the long-term pain of being separated from God.

Jesus once asked a famous question, "What good is it for someone to gain the whole world, yet forfeit their soul?" (Mark 8:36). The answer is obvious—no good. It is no good to trade a few minutes for forever. It is no good to skip out on God's presence, God's Word, God's house, God's people—just to gain something so small by comparison.

Do you understand that? Eternity is eternal. It lasts forever and ever (and ever, hallelujah!).[14] That is why our Savior came into this world—so your forever would not have a single tear or an ounce of regret or a moment of feeling less than. Jesus' cleansing grace gives us an eternity of unimaginable happiness. Sure, kicking a porn habit might bring you closer relationships, but that is nothing compared to what is coming for God's people. We will see the face of God! And every desire and craving and hunger and thirst of our hearts will be fully and supremely met. "Earth has nothing I desire besides you, [God]," Asaph sang (Psalm 73:25), and God is exactly what we have forever because of Jesus Christ.

Perhaps my most powerful (and questionable) illustration of the gospel came from a preacher I once met at a Detroit Lions game. He said there was once a woman who supposedly had a vision where she spoke with Jesus. When she told the members of her church, they informed the pastor, who was concerned. He knew the history of people who claimed to speak directly with God and how quickly such "visions" turned into a higher

---

14 Sorry, I couldn't help myself. And you owe me a dollar if you're humming some Handel right now.

authority than the Bible itself. So, the pastor set up a time to speak with this woman and gently tried to gauge her emotional health. "How have you been feeling, Mary?" he asked. "Anything I can pray for? Any struggles keeping you up at night?" Mary appreciated his concern, but could only smile. "I'm doing amazing, Pastor! I spoke with Jesus last week!"

But the pastor was not convinced. So he decided to put Mary to the test. "Mary," he smiled, "if Jesus ever decides to appear to you again, I want you to ask him a question. Ask Jesus what sin I really struggled with when I was in college." The pastor knew that the only people who knew about that specific sin were himself and God. He didn't expect this "visionary" woman to be the third.

A few weeks passed until the pastor heard the whispers. Another vision. Better than the first one. So once more the pastor and Mary sat down in his office. "Well," he eventually said, "did you ask Jesus my question?" "Oh, yes, Pastor. How could I forget?" Mary grinned. "Really?" the pastor skeptically asked, leaning forward in his chair. "And what did Jesus say?"

"Well, I asked Jesus what sin you really struggled with when you were in college. Jesus paused, looked right back at me, paused again, and said, 'I don't remember.'"

Does that story sound too good to be true? Don't answer before you read Jeremiah: "Declares the LORD, . . . 'I will make a new covenant. . . . I . . . will remember their sins no more'" (Jeremiah 31:31, 34). Say what?!? How can an all-knowing God not remember something? Is God forgetful? Absentminded?

No, God is just that committed to the gospel. Technically, the word "remember" here means to call something to mind in order to act upon it (like when God "remembered" Noah and protected him from the coming flood). So Jeremiah is saying that God will never, ever call our sins to mind in order to act upon them in judgment and condemnation. Yet the very choice of words is meant to communicate that when God thinks about us, our sins do not even cross his mind!

Isn't that the sweetest thing ever? We cannot be so sure about dreams and visions, but we can be positive about passages and revelations! If you are a follower of Jesus, God does not remember your sins. It is as if we confess, "God, I am so sorry I did that again . . . " and God replies, "Did what?" It is as if we cry, "God, I did it again, the thousandth time . . . " and God smiles, "I don't remember the first time." It is as if we stew over our sins, sit in puddles of guilt, rehash our failures, and God walks in, grinning, "You are my child! I love you! With you I am well pleased!"

That love, inexplicable as it is, is what we will enjoy forever. It is what we need so much more than a few steps to a better whatever. I get it. We are addicted to quick fixes. We find it nearly impossible to endure. But fix your eyes on Jesus and you will understand the eternity of pleasure that awaits you, even if porn is your struggle until the day you die. I hope and pray this book helps God's people reject porn and all its consequences, but even if you are in that war until your last breath, you will not regret the fight. One glimpse of God's face and it will all be worth it. You will be dancing before the first measure of heaven's music is over!

But are we not sinners too? Yes, I wish I could say that you stopped being a sinner back at your baptism, but every day has shown that to be far from true. We are, at the same time, sinners and saints. Completely right with God yet completely locked in a battle with our sinful hearts. We look in the mirror and think of a hundred spiritual flaws, but God thinks of none. All he sees, because of the blood of his Son, is a saint. A holy, precious child. A son or a daughter who puts a smile on his face.

**2. THE GOSPEL PROMISES THAT WE CAN DANCE TODAY.** A second reason to start with saving love instead of simple steps is because the gospel says we don't have to wait until eternity to dance. We don't have to mope through this life, punishing ourselves for our sins, proving to God how very sorry we are by not smiling for an appropriate amount of time.

The Scriptures teach repentance, not penance. Repentance means taking the sorrow you feel because of your sin and running with it to Jesus, who cleanses and purifies and makes you holy. Penance is a man-made system to work your way back into an acceptable state of wholeness and purity.

Please do not misunderstand. I am not saying that we should take sin lightly. I am not suggesting you should shrug instead of weeping tears of repentance. But I am saying that the father in Jesus' parable didn't want his dirty son to cry on the dance floor. He saw his tears, heard his confession, and forgave him entirely. The time for sorrow was over. The time for joy was here.

Perhaps you have read the gorgeous words of Lamentations chapter 3. If you are Bible-nerdy,[15] you may be familiar with the line about God's mercy and compassion, but check out the entire section. "I remember my affliction and my wandering, the bitterness and the gall. I well remember them, and my soul is downcast within me. Yet this I call to mind and therefore I have hope: Because of the LORD's great love we are not consumed, for his compassions never fail. They are new every morning; great is your faithfulness" (Lamentations 3:19-23). Jeremiah is saying, "I remember my wandering. It tastes like gall, like bile that has crept up from my guts. That is why my soul is so sad. So I will call this to mind: God has great love for me! He never fails! Every morning there is more compassion! God, you are so faithful!"

That is what you will need "the morning after." So can I ask a personal question? Are you dragging the porn of your past into your present? Are you believing the lie that you are still dirty to God, despite your faith in Jesus? Has Satan tricked you

---

15 I mean that in the best way.

into thinking you could work off your sin by moping around all week? Then call these truths to your mind. Find hope in the promises of God. Jesus won't just make you clean in the future. He has declared you clean right here and right now.

Paul made that same point with the Christians in Galatia. Although he had preached the pure grace of God to them, some new preachers came to town after Paul's departure and "bewitched" these new Christians (Galatians 3:1). What was their spell? Convincing the Galatians that though salvation might start with grace, it ends with works. The Father might give you a push to get you started, but then you have to pedal your bike up the mountain of salvation. "After beginning by means of the Spirit, are you now trying to finish by means of the flesh?" (Galatians 3:3).

You have felt that too, haven't you? You rejoiced that God rescued you by grace. You were dead, but he made you alive. You were blind, but he made you see. You couldn't do anything, so Jesus did everything. But then, as you read more of the Bible and heard more sermons, you learned about the Christian life. You started to understand the commandments. And, somehow, you started to put your peace, your joy, your confidence not in the stress-relieving grace of God but in the stress-inducing obedience of you. The commandments, good and helpful in and of themselves, are so easily twisted into something they were never intended to be. They become our hope, our salvation, our chance to perform our way into God's accepting embrace.

No wonder we don't enjoy the fruit of joy more often. So listen to Paul. Just like Abraham started with faith in Genesis chapter 12 and continued with faith in Genesis chapter 15. Just like the Galatians' hope was all about faith in Jesus at their conversion and still about faith in Jesus years later. It is the same for us. We could dance on the first day we met Jesus, all because of the love and mercy of God. And we can dance today, all because of the love and mercy of God.

**3. THE GOSPEL IS THE BEST "STEP."** The final reason to focus on God's saving work instead of our practical steps is that the gospel works better than we do. It has more power to change us than all of our best checklists and self-help steps combined.

Some have suggested that porn use increases in parts of the country with high levels of church attendance. Why would that be? Perhaps because Christianity so often devolves into a do-it-yourself system of morality? Or because too many people have groaned under a burden of biblical commands that is rarely relieved by the thoroughly beautiful work of Jesus on the cross? The gospel ensures that God's people find rest and relief in Christ, which results in explosive spiritual power.

I think back to a bride-to-be and her fiancé. I'll call them Amanda and Chris. Amanda wanted to change her future husband[16] and she thought she knew how—nagging. She would tell him to change, insist that he change, even threaten him if he didn't change. I suggested there was a better way to do marriage—to change yourself. To choose to put your spouse first all the time. To serve and not want to be served. To submit to each other out of reverence for Christ. To treat him like the Christian church treats Christ.

Amanda wasn't buying it. She pushed back, insisting that if she didn't nag him, he would just keep doing the same selfish stuff for their entire lives. She needed to nag. So I asked her, "How's it working? You've been nagging him for a while now. Is he changing?" Amanda's defensiveness deflated instantly. She sighed, dropped her head, and admitted, "No . . . " I have not seen Amanda or Chris for many years, but I pray that conversation changed the way they treat each other.

What Amanda (and pretty much all of us) forgot was the power of unconditional love. When we are a dirty mess and

---

[16] Ladies, bringing long lists of "Things for Him to Change" to premarriage counseling is a wonderful way to give your pastor job security.

someone loves us, it has a powerful effect on our hearts. It stirs us and changes us from the inside out. When speaking to those "dirty" Corinthians, Paul agreed—"Christ's love compels us, because we are convinced that one died for all, and therefore all died. And he died for all, that those who live should no longer live for themselves but for him who died for them and was raised again" (2 Corinthians 5:14,15). How does God get sinners to no longer live for themselves? He compels them with Christ's love.

The apostle John was on that same page. John was known as that elderly Christian who wrote powerful letters about Christian love. Meditate on 1 John and you will see his unwavering commitment for Christians to love with their words and actions. So where do we find the power to love like that? John says it simply: "We love because [God] first loved us" (1 John 4:19). God's love for you in Christ, the saving love that preceded your first good work, is the same love that fires you up to do good works.

Think back to the dirty son from Jesus' story. Do you think he went back to the filth? Do you think he trampled on his father's love with his new sandals? Do you think he sold that robe and that ring to hook up with the old prostitutes he knew? Do you think he slapped his dad in the face, saying, "Thanks for the steak, Pops. Got any more cash for me?" No, I don't think so. Forgive me for assuming more than the story says, but I can't imagine the kid wanting to go back to his sin. I picture his heart being so overwhelmed by unconditional love that he decided to stay home and dance with his dad.

## Wanna Dance?

Back in 2014, I became the official pastor of a church in Appleton, Wisconsin. The service during which I was officially installed ended in a way I did not expect. The lead vocalist invited me up on stage during a musical interlude and told my new church that I was going to lead us in dancing. Unfortunately, this was pre-Jakey G, and my dance moves were not yet fitting for the public eye. Even more unfortunately, a dozen fellow pastors from Appleton were in attendance, meaning I was about to embarrass myself in front of my colleagues.[17]

Being an extrovert, I played along. I pogo-sticked like a scrawny, 6' 2" Caucasian for a bit, wondering how David felt that day when he busted out his best moves for the Lord. But then the lead vocalist reminded us all where the lyrics of that song came from. The song was a shout-out to Jesus' story about a God who is so good to sinners—sexual sinners included—that he invites them out into the light to dance instead of groveling in the darkness of shame.

I came to love that song, mainly because I love that God. How about you? You might not dance in front of three hundred people, but does your soul jump at the chance to praise God for his mercy? Jesus' pure life, his dirty death, and his cleansing resurrection are all we need to dance today. Trust in him and start dancing!

> Let Israel rejoice in their Maker;
> let the people of Zion be glad in their King.
> Let them praise his name with dancing.
>
> (PSALM 149:2,3)

---

[17] Thankfully, they were Midwestern, conservative, Lutheran pastors whose dancing abilities have been described in a previous footnote.

# 3

# ⅁ꞮꞜꞒꞱꞲ Laundry

I bet you would not want the world to closely examine your undershirts. Those bright white shirts you bought in a three-pack. Because I bet they are not as bleach white as they once were. Whether you are a profuse sweat-er or just lightly perspire, I bet the armpits of your undershirts look like most of ours. A disturbing shade of grey that the millennials call "pit stains."[18]

Needless to say, you will probably not be wearing the aforementioned shirts out in public. You will cover up the proof that you are a sweat-er with a cable knit sweater (and spritz some perfume or cologne over the top).

Because that is what we do. We put out our best in public. We try not to, as the saying goes, air our dirty laundry. The clean laundry, sure. But the dirty stuff? No, that is best kept behind the closed doors of the laundry room.

Which is what most of us think about pornography. Porn is dirty and deserves to be kept behind closed doors. We might use it, but we must not admit to it. We can fight against it, but that battle must be fought alone. After all, what would people say if they knew the dirtiest things about us? What would your parents and siblings and classmates and churchmates think if Jesus-loving, Bible-believing, churchgoing you were also a

---

18 Other people might also call them pit stains, but Christian books sell better when you mention millennials.

porn user? How would they look at you if they knew porn was an issue in your marriage, with your kids, at your church?

We assume we know the answers to those questions. People would be disgusted. Appalled, they would take a step away from us. The shock would blurt out, "You?!? Do that?!?" They wouldn't want to sit next to us in church or pray with us at Bible study. They wouldn't want to be our friend anymore. They would fear guilt by association. They would think less of us, think the worst of us, think they're better than us. So we know what we have to do. We have to cover it all up. We have to go back to war alone, an army of one.

But one doesn't work. Like that YouTube video I saw of a teenager bench-pressing alone in his basement. He starts the video recording, puts on his pump-up music, and gets that heavy breathing going that you hear in the weight room.[19] He lifts the loaded barbell, drops it to his chest, and heaves it back up . . . almost. The momentum stops three quarters of the way back to the rack, and his breathing gets panicked. You cringe as the bar drops to his chest. You see his bulging eyes staring back at the camera. You wonder if you're about to watch a kid die by bench press. Seconds pass as his mind scrambles for options until, finally, he screams, "Dad!" He waits, listens, then squeals, "Mom!"

Call me twisted, but I love that video. I love it not only for its comedic value, but also for the valuable lesson it teaches us about trying to push back against porn by ourselves.

I wish I would have learned that lesson when I started struggling with porn. Terrified to tell anyone, I tried everything except confession. You should have heard my mental reasoning. "I'm just a teenager. After I turn 18 my testosterone will slow down and this won't be a problem." "I'm just single. Once I find a girlfriend, I'll fall in love, and this won't be a problem." "I'm

---

[19] At least I assume you hear such things in weight rooms, but I have not been in one in a while.

just engaged. Once we get married and can enjoy sex, this won't be a problem." I tried 127 versions of "Once I _____, this won't be a problem." But it kept being a problem.

Please don't paint me as a slacker. I was a Bible-reading, Scripture-memorizing, church-attending Christian. I was so intense about my faith that I would drive the speed limit in the left lane of the interstate to help other people to not sin by speeding![20] I once took my entire collection of hip-hop CDs and busted them in my garage with a hammer, convinced that selling them would be to spread a sinful message to others. My senior pictures proudly showcased my WWJD? bracelet. In other words, I was, perhaps, misguided but absolutely intense about my relationship with God.

But the one thing I never, ever did was tell anyone about my porn problem. Not my pastor (and he was a great man). Not my parents (and they are great people). Not my college class-mates (and they were amazing Christians). Nobody. That step was too much. My dirty laundry was mine and mine alone. But it never seemed to get clean. . . .

In my experience, 99 percent of Christians try that approach (give or take 1 percent). We will double our prayer time, triple our Scripture reading, and make a thousand promises to God but not tell a single soul. Often when people confess this sin to me, I'll ask, "How long has this been a struggle?" The answer is typically years, if not over a decade, even for believers in their 20s. Then I'll ask, "Who else knows about this?" Most often, if they haven't been caught by a parent or spouse, the answer is, "Just you, Pastor. I haven't told anyone."

How about you? If porn is your struggle, does anyone know? Is this something you talk about? Or is this book just one more weapon in your army-of-one strategy? I wish I could tell you that this book is good enough to fix it, but I don't think it will. If God's Word didn't "work," why would my words?

[20] In retrospect, I may have led thousands of drivers into temptation. . . .

Like that poor teenager under the barbell, we have pushed as hard as we can, but we can't seem to escape. Maybe the only thing left is to cry out for help.

As it turns out, that is exactly what Jesus was after all along. After his longest sermon, the Sermon on the Mount (which has a famous section on lust, by the way), Jesus concluded, "But everyone who hears these words of mine and does not put them into practice is like a foolish man who built his house on sand. The rain came down, the streams rose, and the winds blew and beat against that house, and it fell with a great crash" (Matthew 7:26,27). Did you catch that? You can hear Jesus' words and still crash. You can come to church every Sunday and turn your home into a devotional sanctuary and still crash. We are all one storm away from a great crash if we do not put Jesus' words into practice.

That truth forces me to do two things. First, it forces me to run back to Jesus, for who of us, even on our best days, puts all of God's Word into practice? Second, it forces me to think about the blessings of obedience.

I wish I could rewind to my freshman year of high school, the year before my struggle intensified, and tell myself to obey two passages—Proverbs 28:13 and James 5:16. I wish I would have done more than check the box to prove I read them. I wish I had put God's wisdom into practice. Let's explore both of those passages in depth.

Proverbs 28:13 says, "Whoever conceals their sins does not prosper, but the one who confesses and renounces them finds mercy." According to Solomon, the wisest man on planet Earth, you don't prosper (aka succeed, get ahead, blossom, or progress) if you conceal your sins.

That is certainly true with God. Trying to hide your sins from God robs you of the chance to hear his merciful response. "If we confess our sins, he is faithful and just and will forgive us our sins and purify us from all unrighteousness" (1 John 1:9).

But that is also true with others. Concealing our sins from those who love us will cost us. When we choose to fight in the dark, we find ourselves swinging madly, without landing a solid punch. When we choose to stay in the shadows, we don't produce the fruit that grows in the light of community. When we refuse to confess our sins openly, we rob others of the chance to remind us that God's mercy is new every morning.

Jump to the New Testament, and James will tell you the same thing as Solomon. James 5:16 commands and promises, "Therefore confess your sins to each other and pray for each other so that you may be healed. The prayer of a righteous person is powerful and effective." Confess your sins. Not sin in general like you sometimes do in church, but sins in particular like we rarely do . . . well, ever. Why? So that you may be healed. So that you may be cured like Jesus cured people of their crippling illnesses. How does such healing happen? By the prayers of others. James has an army-of-some instead of an army-of-one view of sanctification. We all need a band of brothers and sisters to fight our sins with their prayers.

This is more than a onetime, blurt-it-out kind of confession. In the original Greek of the New Testament, James says, "Keep on confessing your sins to one another." This is not a swallow-hard-and-get-it-over-with box to check. No, this is a habit, a lifestyle, a life lived in the light of honest confession with trusted and forgiving friends.

I adore these passages because I have seen their power firsthand. For me, it was April 24th. That was the day that I went to see a counselor. Looking back, I laugh at how unimpressive it all was. On paper, the counselor and I were not a good fit. I have a fire hose for a mouth, an extrovert who always has too much to say. He was an introvert with more facial hair than words. I don't remember any revolutionary counseling insights or practical steps that saved me from my addiction. I just remember confessing instead of concealing. I remember him listening and not judging. And, God be praised, that practice had power, more power than all my promises and private prayers combined. I thank God for that man!

At Conquerors through Christ, the purity ministry I help lead, we have seen my story replayed dozens of times. Sexual sinner reaches out for help. We tell sexual sinner the gospel. We tell sexual sinner to confess to others. Sexual sin radically decreases. It's not always that simple, but often it is. Airing our dirty laundry has the power to cleanse it, as if the fresh breeze of Christian community has purifying power.

But wait. What about their reactions? What about the awkward expressions when you put Solomon's and James' words into practice? You can't exactly put that toothpaste back in the tube, so what if you confess your struggle with porn and immediately regret it?

Here is my answer: The consequences of confession are less. Are there occasionally consequences for those who confess? Do spouses sometimes get angry? Do marriages sometimes end? Do immature listeners sometimes violate your confidence? Do those who are blind to their own sin think you are a worse sinner than they are? Do ministers and their ministries need to be evaluated? Sure. I can't promise there won't be consequences to your confession.

Yet I am convinced the consequences of confession are less. I have yet to meet a single person who has taken this step and regretted it. That is not an exaggeration. Not a single person has told me, "Mike, I did that confession thing you told me to do, and you were so wrong! I wish I would have kept it a secret." No one says that. Instead, they find surprising reactions, allies in the fight, and mercy freely given. Because Solomon wasn't stupid (nor was the Holy Spirit who inspired him!) You find mercy when you stop concealing your sins.

Doesn't it work that way when someone confesses to you? I asked that question at a recent men's conference to 150 men, most of whom I had never met. The topic of the day was sexual satisfaction in marriage, and I opened up about my sexual sins. There I was in front of pastors, Christian teachers, and church leaders, confessing the shameful parts of my past.

After all my dirty laundry was billowing in the air, I asked them, "Do you guys think less of me? Are you disgusted by me? Tempted to take a step away from me?" They immediately shook their heads. One guy, an author who has written a brilliant book about effective public speaking, raised his hand. "You're modeling confession for us," he said. Even more, they were modeling the most common reaction God's people have to sexual sinners—grace.

Isn't Paul the proof of that? My favorite section of Scripture is perhaps the most vulnerable in the entire Book. While Paul doesn't specify his sins, he is brutally honest about his struggle. He confesses to the Romans, "I do not understand what I do. For what I want to do I do not do, but what I hate I do. So I find this law at work: Although I want to do good, evil is right there with me. For in my inner being I delight in God's law; but I see another law at work in me, waging war against the law of my mind and making me a prisoner of the law of sin at work within me. What a wretched man I am!" (Romans 7:15,21-24). Paul didn't pen that confession the day after his conversion but 25 years after meeting Jesus. Even after writing books of the Bible, including passages about purity, Paul still knew the dirty feeling of being a wretched sinner.

So do you hate Paul after reading that? Do you think he is a hypocrite unworthy of your time? Do you want to slam the Bible shut and run away from Paul because of all his sinful baggage? No, I would guess you don't. I bet you are a lot like me, drawn to this section because you can relate to it. The consequence of Paul's confession is closeness. Instead of running away from him, you relate to him, draw nearer to him.

In a healthy spiritual community, others will do the same to you. The Holy Spirit is powerfully working in and through God's people, and the vast majority of them would still love you, pray for you, and walk with you, no matter how dirty your sexual sin might be. As one man put it, "When you talk about your strengths, you create competition. When you talk about your weaknesses, you create community."

Can you imagine if we did that? What if your church was not a place of competition, not a place where you feared judgment and, therefore, kept spiritual secrets? What if your church was a place of . . . love? What if you confessed and people cared? What if they wanted to pray, to help, to walk with you, to remind you of the grace of God? What if the gathering of God's people was not about looking good but about getting better as we truly walk together to the cross? What if the church was the place you sprinted to after your sin because you knew what you would find there? Mercy. Love. Help. Community. A reason to dance again.

I know that is a massive step for most of our churches. But it is a step worth taking. And it only happens when we stop hiding from one another, when we fear missing out on the blessings of confession more than we fear the consequences of it.

## Dos and Don'ts of Dirty Laundry

So if you are convinced it is time to come clean and confess, what should you do? Here are a few quick dos and don'ts when it comes to confessing your sins and hearing the confessions of others:

**Do find accountability partners (plural).** While a trusted friend is essential for frequent confession and encouragement, you will need more than one person to escape your porn habit. Why? Because your friend is not God. During times of temptation, you will need someone to text, to talk you off the ledge, and—unless your friend, like Jesus, is "with you always" and, like God, "never slumbers nor sleeps"—you may need a backup plan.

But turn your accountability partner into your accountability partners, and you'll find the availability that you need. In a world where most of us have our phones with us frequently, the odds are high of reaching at least one friend in a group text. When you sense that a seed of temptation has been planted (an emotional frustration or the thought of acting out), send an immediate cry for help. With enough encouragers in your corner, you will find the help you need.

If you had to choose three people, who would they be? A friend from church? One of your siblings? Your small group Bible study leader? A colleague? An old friend? Pick your top three, and reach out to them today. You will not regret it!

**Don't choose cops or coaches.** Author Michael Cusick explains the dangers of believing that all accountability is created equally. It is not. Some people are like cops, who police behavior with threats. They will encourage you when you do well and scold you when you don't. But the law only motivates us for a little while. Our hearts need more than justice. They need justification in Jesus' name.

Slightly better, but not quite sufficient, are coaches who give you tips to do better next time. They pull you aside, help you see what you did wrong, and offer some solid advice to improve. While more compassionate than the cops, coaches specialize in steps instead of salvation.

So what other type of accountability is there? Answer: Christian. Those who, as Solomon said, help confessors find mercy. The same people who, as James pointed out, pray for us so that we may be healed. Like cops, their frequent check-ins might deter us from sin. Like coaches, they will have good advice when we need it. But like Christ, they will specialize in the proclamation of God's love for us, even after we fall into sin.

As you think about your list of names from above, who "gets" grace? Who loves Jesus, knowing that Jesus loves them? Who understands what it's like to struggle with sin enough to be less judgmental and more compassionate? Those people will become your best allies in the fight.

At the Bible study that meets in my living room, we strive for that kind of Christian accountability. We work hard to be real, to reveal the "real us" instead of the "Facebook us." Yet even after years of open confession, it can still be scary to admit the ugly stuff. So we have a habit of responding to personal confessions with a standard question—you know that God loves you, right? We want the first word spoken to a confessing sinner to be a gospel word, a word of absolution and forgiveness.

**Do tell your significant other.** If you are dating, engaged, or married, it is important to let your significant other in on your secret. Back in grade school we learned, "Secrets, secrets are no fun. Secrets, secrets hurt someone." That is true. Secret sins hurt people. Therefore, bring them into the light, confess your struggle, and ask for forgiveness.

If you take that step this week, can I offer two quick tips? First, explain that you are sharing the news because you want to love your wife/husband/etc. better. Say something like, "Honey, I know this hurts to hear, but I am telling you because I don't want to hurt you anymore. I want to get better, to love you better, and keeping this a secret is only making this worse." Help them to see the heart behind the confession that might hurt.

Second, take a few steps before this one. If you can enter this conversation with proof of your desire to change, you will provide hope to your hurting loved one. Ideally, you will want to say something like, "Sugarbumpkins,[21] I really want to love you better and never look at porn again. That's why I set up an appointment to talk to our pastor and I've read this book and I've installed a filter on my phone and I've asked two friends to keep me accountable." Steps like these convince your loved one that you are walking the walk and not just talking the talk.

**Don't expect your significant other to be happy.** The enemy often sabotages our recovery with false expectations. Perhaps you have decided to take my advice and tell others that you need help. For years, you have been struggling in the darkness and now, by God's grace, you are ready to step into the light. You are happy, even excited about the potential of Solomon's and James' promises. So you share the news.

And your significant other is not happy. Things turn cold. She batters you with questions. He shies away from the intimacy you rightly crave. Things seem to be getting worse instead of better. Huh? Was confession a mistake?

In that moment, please try to walk in your significant other's shoes. They have been sinned against, lied to, deceived, and digitally cheated on hundreds, if not thousands, of times. You have chosen to look at strangers' bodies instead of your spouse's body. Sin, by its very nature, separates people, and your sin has separating power too.

Warning—this might have consequences. No one enjoys finding out they have been sexually sinned against, so prepare yourself for frustration, confusion, and questions. It is natural and is to be expected. In fact, depending on the details of your situation, your relationship might be in danger. The lies that surround porn use can erode the bedrock of trust that every relationship requires. Jesus made it clear that lust is a form of adultery, and many people feel like they have been cheated on when they learn of their lover's porn use.

---

21 If "Sugarbumpkins" isn't your preferred pet name, feel free to insert a replacement.

I admit that this is subjective soil. I do not believe that every wife whose husband has looked at porn has a God-given right to divorce. Nor do I believe that every husband whose wife has read a steamy romance novel can file divorce papers with a clean conscience.

However, there are cases where the addiction, the lies, the lack of trust, and the wounds are so deep that the marriage needs some serious evaluation. A counselor and a pastor might need to get involved to help answer the challenging questions about the future. There may, indeed, be a biblical reason to end the marriage. Porn kills. Marriages are, unfortunately, no exception.

No matter how those questions are answered, however, you will need to work hard to prove yourself trustworthy and to rebuild what your sin has damaged.

So remember Paul's timeless words: "Love is patient" (1 Corinthians 13:4). Be patient as your significant other passes through stages of anger and grief and denial. Ask God for strength to endure those hard days, trusting that they are labor pains that will bring new life to your relationship within a few months. Don't criticize the sadness or blame your partner for making the stage harder. Love "is not proud" either (1 Corinthians 13:4). It humbly confesses and trusts God to work out his plans at his chosen time.

At this point, you might be questioning the wisdom of this entire chapter. "Mike, if that could happen, why would I take the chance? Why would I risk my relationship or my family when I might be able to fix this on my own?"

That is a raw and real question. Here is my answer—because it will only get worse. Unless Proverbs was way off, those who conceal their sins will not prosper. In fact, if your past is any indication of your future, then this struggle will get darker and darker over time. There might be some consequences now, but they will be far less than the consequences you will face later on, if you decide to go back into hiding. The deception will lead to darkness. The darkness will inch you closer to death.

So, brother, let me beg you. Sister in Christ, let me plead with you. Own your sin and its consequences. Keep confessing it to other people. Trust that this is the road to greatest blessing, even if the way seems dark and narrow for the moment.

**Do sign up for protective software.** I once heard of a woman who had a terrible shopping addiction. She knew she shouldn't self-medicate her boredom and sadness with retail therapy, but some days the mall seemed to magnetically pull her into the parking lot. Before she knew it, she was swiping her credit card and squeezing her bags into her trunk.

So she tried a radical idea. Grabbing a mixing bowl, she filled it with water and plunged her credit cards inside. Sticking the bowl in the freezer, she waited until her spending options were frozen beneath two inches of solid ice. Then she made herself a deal. If she was tempted to shop, she would take out the bowl and wait until the ice melted down to her credit cards.

What do you think? Smart idea? Sure, it wasn't a foolproof way to never shop again, but it was a way to make her addiction difficult, giving her heart time to think instead of tunneling down the same path to compulsive behavior.

Filters and accountability software work the same way. Do internet filters make finding porn impossible? No. Can a porn addict figure out alternative search words to find sinful content? Sure. But will the right software slow down a search long enough to give the Holy Spirit time to guide us? Absolutely.

Filters, as their name implies, filter out questionable websites. They block words that are commonly associated with searches of sexual nature. Accountability software sends a report of all the websites you have visited to a designated accountability partner.[22] Some products, like those sold by Covenant Eyes (the filter/accountability software that I use), do both. You can find a list of popular products along with our team's personal reviews at www.conquerorsthroughchrist.net.

In my experience, these products are powerful. While there are much better reasons to avoid porn than embarrassment, sometimes embarrassment is what works in the moment. I have faced temptation, one small search away from sin, and thought, "I don't want to explain this to my friend...." Like a credit card in ice, that pause was what I needed to flee from sexual sin.

**Don't let software excuse the hard work.** Have you ever met someone who took a weight loss supplement and expected to lose weight? They slather an inch of butter on toxic white bread, pour salt on even the healthiest veggies, and count watching sports as their exercise for the month. Then they pop a pill and wait for infomercial-esque results. To no one's surprise, the six-pack doesn't magically appear the next morning.

In the same way, installing Covenant Eyes won't give you covenant eyes. Job explained, "I made a covenant with my eyes not to look lustfully at a young woman" (Job 31:1). But that covenant promise did not mean Job was exempt from the hard work of avoiding the second, lustful look. He had to fight temptation, to bounce his eyes, to recall the right passages at the right time, to stay away from alluring people and places. The covenant was a supplement, not a hard work replacement.

Satan still wins if you are a lazy subscriber to accountability software. The devil is delighted if you have a filter but no fight in you. But the angels cheer when those supplements actually supplement your battle plan versus porn. If being alone at night when you're enjoying a glass of wine is your trigger for trouble, don't expect your filter settings to save you. Be ready to work

---

22 Please remember that all searches are reported, even nonsexual ones. So if you spent an entire afternoon watching cat videos, a trusted friend will discover your dirtiest secret.

hard with your accountability partner, and let your filter be your backup plan.

**Do dig deeper into sexual sins.** There is a difference between checking a box and checking your heart. When I first started an accountability partnership with a friend, I would check a series of boxes each week. I tried to list all the things that could mess up my life and my ministry. Am I serving my wife? Am I giving generously? How many alcoholic drinks did I have this week? Did I look at porn? How many hours did I sleep each night? Am I avoiding any tense relationships? Etc. Each week, I would open up the checklist and give an honest report.

That was a big step for me. Never before had I been that accountable to another human being. Instead of the vague and unhelpful, "How was your week?" questions, the specificity of my checklist revealed any sins or struggles with no way to avoid an honest confession.

But I quickly learned that there was something even better than this big step. Even better than checking a box was checking my heart. Better than asking, "Did I?" was asking, "Why did I?" Why did I fail to love my wife in concrete ways this week? What happened? What was I doing instead? These questions allowed me to see triggers for my sins and patterns that I could avoid with the help of God and my accountability partner.

This is the beautifully painful part of Christian accountability. Allow a friend to dig deeper, to follow the bad fruit back to its rotten root, to help you deal with the disease and not just the symptoms. Often, porn is just a cover for something else. It might be a struggling marriage or depression or feeling powerless at work. It could be loneliness or anger or boredom late at night. Therefore, leverage your trusted friends and dig deeper. You won't regret it.

**Don't forget about the power of the gospel.** I love the people God put in Pastor Max Lucado's life. The well-known Christian author once told the story of a secret he revealed to the leaders of his church. With a family history of alcoholism, Lucado had vowed to never drink, to never tempt his predisposed genes. But after years of 0.00, he got the itch. Nothing extreme, just a beer. But he didn't want to drink at home where his family would see him. And he didn't want to drink at the bar where he might pull up a seat next to a member of his church. So for a week straight, Lucado found himself in a gas station parking lot, secretly sipping a single beer out of a paper bag. But the cover-up didn't work with God. Lucado felt a heavy hand pushing down on his conscience, and he knew the hypocrisy wasn't in tune with the Holy Spirit. So he threw the beer out, scheduled a meeting with his church's elders, and confessed. He didn't lie. He didn't excuse. He just sang a sad song of confession. And when the sad song was done, one of the elders reached out a hand and set it on Lucado's shoulder. He looked the shamed pastor in the eye and said, "What you did was wrong. But what you're doing is right. God's love is great enough to cover your sin."

Yes! That is exactly what to say when the post-confession silence is thick in the air. Acknowledge the sin. Then exalt the Savior. God's love is enough. His grace is sufficient. His mercy is exponentially greater than our struggles. "Where sin increased, grace increased all the more" (Romans 5:20).

Friends, please believe that the gospel is what we need. We don't move past it, but deeper into it. True spiritual growth happens when God's love sinks so deeply into our soul that we are satisfied without sin. A life without porn happens when God is so glorious to us that the short-term bursts of dopamine can't compete with his presence in our lives. So preach the good news to yourself and to one another.

These eight dos/don'ts are far from an exhaustive list, but they are a great place to start. No accountability relationship is perfect, and you will learn as you go. But it is far better to take a good step now than to spend the next year figuring out a perfect step. Trust that God will prosper your confession and that the prayers of those who hear of your sin are powerful and effective enough to heal you.

## Dirty Laundry at Church?

Some of you reading this book are pastors and Christian teachers. Others of you serve on church leadership teams or facilitate small group Bible studies. If that describes you, I have two urgent things you need to consider.

First, you are not this chapter's exemption. If you are a pastor with a porn problem, you will not prove Solomon wrong. Pastors who conceal their sins will not prosper. If you teach kids about the Savior but have a secret sin, James is also talking to you. Confess that secret to others so that you can be healed.

In fact, spiritual leaders are Satan's target market for impurity. I recall sitting in a Kwik Trip parking lot,[23] listening to a sexual addiction counselor laugh at my honest question. I had asked him, "Why does it seem that so many pastors struggle with pornography?" When his laughter died down, he explained, "Because they are pastors!"

Duh, Mike. Strike the shepherd and the sheep will scatter. Make the minister keep secrets, and the members will follow. Turn porn into something taboo, and God's people will zip their lips and try to pray their porn away. The counselor's comment made perfect sense. If I were Satan, I would do the same thing.

Combine the devil's targeted schemes with long hours, plenty of time with a computer, stressful work conditions, too many nights away from family, and a fear of the consequences

---

[23] Kwik Trip, if you are unfamiliar, is the best gas station on planet Earth, famous for tempting you at the register with delicious cookies at a shockingly reasonable price.

of confession, and you have the perfect recipe for church leaders who fight alone.

Every survey of pastors that I have read reveals the statistics we all wish were not true. According to the Barna Group's massive 2016 study, released in a book titled *The Porn Phenomenon*, 41 percent of senior pastors admit that porn has been a struggle at some point in their lives. Seventeen percent confess that the struggle is current and not past. The numbers increased when youth pastors were surveyed.

If that is you, I want you to know I am typing these next words as slowly and seriously as I can—God delights in you. Read those four words again. God delights in you. Your Father is not embarrassed by you. Your Abba adores you. Your picture is 8x10'd above his fireplace. Your smile shows up on the wallpaper of his phone. God is not disgusted with you, because all who are "baptized into Christ have clothed [themselves] with Christ" (Galatians 3:27).

And I want you to get help. Before this gets worse, before there is a scandal, before the consequences compound, get help. Reach out to a counselor, a brother in the ministry, a brother in the family. Don't drop a confessional bomb in your next sermon. That is neither helpful for the flock nor wise, but do confess. You believe in the power of prayer, so let God's people pray for you. The real you. The you that keeps doing the very things you hate. And you will be healed.

As I mentioned before, there might be consequences. Depending on the severity of your struggle, you will have to think deeply about your current place in ministry. Sometimes porn interrupts work days, meaning pastors are robbing God's people of valuable time. Sometimes porn happens on work devices, meaning a scandal is a single computer crash or pop-up away from happening. Sometimes porn wrecks the pastor's family and they need an intense time of sabbath rest to heal and rebuild what sin has broken. Sometimes to do the good works that God has lined up for us tomorrow, we need to stop what we are doing today. Paul's list of standards for those who oversee God's people (1 Timothy 3:1-7) is as essential for ministry today as it was when he originally wrote it. Sin can, sadly, disqualify a man from his position, breaking hearts in the process. Including his own.

Is this the case with every pastor caught up in porn? No. Is this the case for some? Yes. So let me repeat myself: The consequences of confession are always less. Trust that the Holy Spirit was not lying to you when he carried Solomon and James along as they wrote those challenging words. He wants the best for you. He has your coming days in his hands. So do not be afraid to obey your Lord. God has plans to give you hope and a future, no matter how painful the process of pruning may be.

Second, if you lead any type of ministry, please make it safe. Make your church, your school, your small group, and your family a safe place for porn users. By "safe" I mean creating the kind of atmosphere where it feels less threatening to talk about taboo subjects without fear of judgment, condemnation, or rejection. How do you do that? Let me suggest a few things to keep in mind:

We make it safe when we talk about porn. Avoiding uncomfortable issues is the fuel for addictions. Our silence as pastors and teachers teaches more than we imagine. God's people are taught, "We don't talk about this around here. People who struggle with this, like me, don't belong." We would never say that, but that is what we are saying when we don't say anything about porn. So speak up. Worry more about your struggling brothers and sisters than old Mabel's disgust or a protective father's opinion about the little ears in church. Mabel doesn't know that three of her grandkids are addicted. The father forgets that his little girls have probably already been exposed via a curious classmate on the playground. Be wise when you speak up, but please say something.

Recently, I got an email from a man who told me he did not feel comfortable or "even welcomed" talking to his pastors about pornography. What shocked me about the story was (1) the man did not even have a personal problem with porn— he just wanted advice as he kids were getting older; and (2) the man's pastors are kind, approachable, gospel-loving men. His email made me think about the assumptions people make about their pastors. Unless they have clear evidence to the contrary, they will assume that the church is not a safe place to talk about this topic. So I encourage you to talk candidly about porn with your church family. That will make it a safe place to fight the good fight together.

We make it safe when we talk about *our* church's struggle with porn. Implying that porn is a problem "out there" among "those people" is a wickedly powerful sermon, emphasis on the "wicked." While we certainly want to paint porn as the villain that it is, we must confess that people who love Jesus can fall in love with porn. If our pulpit-pounding and stern classroom lectures only lament the impurity of the world, we push hurting people away from the essential step of confession. Therefore, remind your students that *our Christian* school is filled with liars and gossips and porn users and proud competitors and every type of sinner. Porn is *our* struggle, *our* enemy, *our* concern—because porn is affecting *us*.

We make it safe when we include all demographics. A concerned Christian principal knew he needed to address the porn problem. So he divided the upper graders by gender and asked two teachers to give the "talk" about porn. The boys heard about the struggle many visually oriented young men have with porn. The girls heard about the struggle many visually oriented young men have with porn. And the eighth-grade girl who loved to look at porn felt so sinful she forgot to breathe.

Have you been there? The sermon illustration is about a "wife" who finds her "husband's" internet history, but never vice versa. The marriage seminar implies that men want sex and women put up with sex to please their husbands. The porn warnings are directed at the parents of sons, assuming our daughters would never struggle with that!

But that is a dangerous stereotype. While the statistics are not (yet) equal, nearly 1/3 of porn users are women. The odds are that a significant number of women in your church have looked at porn. Many of them masturbate frequently. And if we act like that doesn't happen, we fail to create a safe place for confession. When we watch our pronouns, we produce a safe environment.

We make it safe when we share our church's stories. Imagine coming to church and hearing the pastor say this: "A young woman came to my office the other day and told me about her porn problem. She was visibly nervous, but she shouldn't have been. Lots of people here at our church struggle with purity. Men and women. Young and old. I was so proud of her for having the wisdom and courage to reach out for help. And I told her what I tell everyone who struggles with porn—you know God loves you, right? We came up with a plan to fight for purity, a plan to keep her connected to other Christian women, but more than anything else I told her that God loves porn users. Jesus died for porn addicts. Porn might be a big struggle here at our church, but when we fight together with prayer and forgiveness, we can win."

In that one little paragraph, what was communicated? Lots! In less than 60 seconds, that pastor made his church a safe place for porn users. He normalized the struggle and let every person know that his church is the perfect place to run to for help and for God's grace. Sharing our stories, the stories of the brothers and sisters right here in our congregation, creates safety in sanctifying amounts.

I know it is easier for me to give this advice. I'm an extrovert who loves talking about tough topics. I have a personal hatred of pornography, a passion to help others with purity, and a stack of 40 books that I have read on the topic. You might be an introverted follower of Jesus who has never struggled and knows little about the subject. But I am pleading with you to think of the statistics. Every Sunday when you preach, there are plenty of people who are withering under the weight of their sexual guilt. Every year when you teach, there are kids who have had a summer of graphic exposure, and they are confused and interested and ashamed. Every week we meet people who the devil is planning to lure into porn's trap for the very first time. Those precious souls need us. They need you to make it safe.

So say something. Even if it's not the perfect something, you never know the souls you will save from a life of porn by your honest efforts to make it safe.

## Why Display the Dirt?

Why am I pushing you so hard to personally confess and create a culture of confession? Because confession is good for our souls. Scripture says it. My pastoral experience supports it. My own story backs it.

In the end, I want our stories to end up like "Jeremy's." Jeremy was caught in porn. He couldn't trust himself with an internet connection and an empty house. He hated what he was doing, but he couldn't find the strength to stop. So he confessed. He told his girlfriend. He told me. And something changed. Here's how Jeremy described it: "When I look back at the transformation in my life, I am blown away. A year ago, I couldn't be alone in my house without falling into temptation. Now, I've been home alone more than I can count and have never even been tempted to fall back to where I had been. It's amazing what happens when you open up and tell someone. I had just accepted it as part of my life, and it doesn't have to be that way. It doesn't have to be something you constantly fall back into and feel ashamed. . . . Telling [my girlfriend] was *by far* the most difficult conversation we have had . . . but it was definitely a turning point in our relationship."

I love that story. Jeremy admits that the conversation was extremely difficult. But, to quote our forgiven brother, "It's amazing what happens when you open up and tell someone." Amen!

When Jeremy slipped and fell back into this sin, I told him to keep confessing. He did and wrote me, "I talked to my fiancé about what happened. It was not an easy conversation, but she was very forgiving and much more understanding of the struggle than the first time she found out."

I love the safety that woman created—she was very forgiving and much more understanding. Amen, sister!

The last email I got from Jeremy was short and sweet: "It's been such a blessing to be more free over the past 18 months than I ever had been."

I love that word—*free*. Amen, Jesus! That is the best reason of all to air our dirty laundry.

# 4

# Dance Steps

Learning to dance is awkward. I remember trying to learn how to wave, a move where an invisible force seems to "wave" through your body from fingertip to fingertip. According to the tutorial, the wave is only five steps. So clear out the furniture and give it a try!

**Step 1:** Hold your arms straight out to your sides. Check! You are 20 percent of the way there!

**Step 2:** Point the fingers of one hand up to the ceiling. Check! Dancing is easy!

**Step 3:** Point those same fingers down as your wrist pops up. Check! At this point, you might be feeling like a Christian version of Poppin' John.[24]

**Step 4:** Push your wrist down until your hand appears to be pushing down on an invisible table and pop your elbow up to the ceiling. Um, not checked. . . . How do you do that? Why don't my arms twist like that?

**Step 5:** Without moving your hand, "push" your elbow toward your shoulder. What? Definitely not checked. Do I look like a Russian gymnast? How does that even work?

---

[24] Not to be confused with Papa John, who is excellent at making pizzas but whose waving skills are unknown.

If you are anything like I was, you should be feeling like an uncoordinated idiot, realizing that those simple steps are not so simple. Slightly embarrassed, you might be tempted to say, "This is stupid," and go back to whatever it is you do well.

But what you should not forget is God's brilliant invention called muscle memory. Ever heard of it? God made our muscles to remember what we repeat. What starts out awkward ends up awesome if you keep repeating the steps.

Thankfully, I didn't give up on waving. I kept pushing my elbow into that awkward position until one day, it didn't seem awkward. Now if I'm ever in a dark alley in Bangkok and am challenged to a dance-off to the death,[25] I will wave my way to survival. Thanks, muscle memory!

The fight against porn is a lot like dancing. There are some basic steps, but they are awkward at first. Like any lifestyle change or new habit, you'll need to persevere through the awkward, uncomfortable days until your spiritual muscles develop a new memory.

In this chapter, I am going to share lots of "steps" to keep in step with the self-controlled Spirit. Some of them, like the first few steps of waving, will be easy. Others, like that weird elbow thing, will seem impossible at first. All of them, if you persevere, will be awesome in the end.

So as a porn-hating (chapter 1), gospel-loving (chapter 2), dirty laundry-airing (chapter 3) follower of Jesus, are you ready to learn some steps?

## H.E.A.L.T.H.

Sarah hadn't planned on looking at porn. She was too busy with her real estate business to think about anything besides

---

[25] I have an upcoming trip to Thailand, so I need to be prepared just in case.

her next showing. Running from one appointment to the next, answering one email after another, working through the lunch hour, Sarah hadn't given a second of thought to anything explicit all day. By the time she got back to her apartment, she was exhausted. And that's when she looked at porn.

Juan didn't plan on porn either. In fact, he hadn't felt the tug of temptation all day. He was too consumed with his struggling marriage for that. Before he could even make it out the door for his morning run, his wife was arguing about the financial mess they were in. Stressed and overwhelmed, Juan skipped his workout, called the credit card company during his lunch, and didn't get home until his wife was already in bed. And that's when he looked at porn.

Have you been there? Porn, somehow, just happens. You weren't searching for it or tiptoeing the line of inappropriate websites (like the sports page that just so happens to have a section of bikinied women . . . ). You were doing well, staying pure, fighting the good fight, but then . . . fail. And you wondered how it even happened.

Those who study addictions believe there are explanations to Sarah's and Juan's struggles. No, they didn't download porn during work or flirt with a coworker at lunch. But they did make a few simple choices that left them weak and vulnerable, easy prey for the predator we call porn. They forgot about their H.E.A.L.T.H.

H.E.A.L.T.H. is an acronym that stands for Hungry, Energy, Angry, Lonely, Tired, and Heart. While many of those words might seem more physical than spiritual, they all have a powerful impact on the spiritual decisions we make regarding pornography. Let's explore each of these steps as we seek to honor God with our bodies.

## HUNGRY

I once met a bride-to-be who confessed one of her biggest struggles to me. It wasn't porn or a scandalous sexual past. "Pastor," she admitted, "I get . . . hangry."

Have you heard of the term *hangry*—when feeling hungry makes you angry? If not, I bet you have felt it. When you skip breakfast and work swallows up your lunch and your head starts to ache and your stomach starts to groan and you find a sharpness to your tongue that wasn't there before.

Think of how hunger connects to what the apostle Paul said about the Christian life. "The fruit of the Spirit is love, joy, peace, forbearance, kindness, goodness, faithfulness, gentleness and self-control" (Galatians 5:22,23). I'm not sure about you, but I'm not sure that gentle and kind and loving best describe me when I'm hungry. So it seems that the "fruit of the Spirit" is connected to eating actual fruit, as opposed to empty-calorie fruit snacks!

It took me 35 years to realize that truth. I was the perpetually skinny guy who many suspected to be hosting a tapeworm. I should have bought stock in frozen pizzas because I would demolish three a week (along with a calorie-packed IPA and a bar of dark chocolate). Three thousand calories after 10 P.M. was the norm in my world. My wife[26] questioned my dietary choices. "You're skinny on the outside," she insisted, "but probably fat on the inside." That's where she got my new nickname—Skinny Fat.

So one day I asked the doctor to confirm her theory. We did blood work and charted my vitals, looking for my inner health. Guess what we found? More skinny! Ha! Take that, Honey! And let's go get some McNuggets!

But there was one vital thing I was forgetting—my behavior. Sure, I could devour a frozen pizza with extra salt and not gain a

---

[26] Inflamed by pure jealousy . . .

pound, but could I binge without bad behavior? Without being lazy? Without falling into a food coma instead of using my creative energy to love my wife and kids? Ummm . . . well . . . man, I hate it when my wife is right. I eventually learned that my body is connected to my soul. My faith is connected to my food. My love is connected to my lunch.

Could porn work the same way? Could a bad diet lead to a bad decision online? Could a fast-food, obese-portion-sized lifestyle leave us sugar-crashed and lazy when we need to be fleeing from sexual temptation?

I know this isn't a dieting book, but maybe a healthy diet that honors the way God wired the human body could give you the extra strength you need to say "No!" to porn. Maybe a high-protein breakfast and a healthy lunch are allies that will help you enjoy a porn-free night after dinner. Maybe an honest conversation with some fitness-minded friends could be another tool God uses to fix your late-night snacking on impurity. Maybe planning better meals is one more way to plan to be pure.

For some of you, that will be an awkward step. You might hate mornings and prefer to sleep in and skip breakfast. You might despise packing a lunch and choose another value meal with your coworkers. Your brain might crave sugar's dopamine-releasing effects. Be ready for the awkwardness, the discomfort of creating a new habit. Remember that the work is worth it. Because not being Hungry is the first step in enjoying sexual H.E.A.L.T.H.

### ENERGY

Have you ever heard of the "runner's high"? That euphoric zone of pleasure despite all the miles of pain. Crossing the finish line after a long run triggers an explosion of dopamine in the brain. I've embraced total strangers in moments like that, which would be awkward if they weren't feeling the same high.

What in the world does that have to do with porn? Well, perhaps we can fight pleasure with pleasure. Instead of letting porn corner the market on the pleasure chemicals in our brains, we should find godly ways to have the same experience.

The apostle Paul told young pastor Timothy, "Physical training is of some value, but godliness has value for all things" (1 Timothy 4:8). Paul's main point was to exalt the value of godliness, but did you catch what he said about fitness? It is "of some value." Paul knew there are good reasons to get in a good workout.

Google "benefits of exercise" and you'll find the research to prove what you've already heard. Regular exercise improves physical and mental and emotional health. It increases energy and helps battle depression. And, if addiction experts are correct, it helps battle compulsive behavior like porn.

So what could you do? Join a gym with a friend? Pick up that sport you used to love in high school? Find your local running club? Go on a morning walk with some girlfriends? (That line was only for women; guys, if you have girlfriends, plural, you need to read this book twice.) Or, kill two birds with one stone and work out with your accountability partners. Hit the gym or play basketball with the friends who are helping you fight against porn.

For some of us, taking the first step to physical fitness will be hard. But those first steps will soon turn into a gazelle stride that brings our brains the high that might protect us from the lows of turning to porn. Because having Energy is the second step in enjoying sexual H.E.A.L.T.H.

### ANGRY

If I would have been 18, his parents might have pressed charges. But I was only in seventh grade, and the police were rarely called to the roller hockey rink. Back in the mid-90s, roller hockey was all the rage,[27] and so my friends and I joined a league.

A few weeks into the season, however, we played the most talented and dirtiest team in the league. One dude spent the whole game hacking at my legs with his stick. At one point, he jacked me between the legs in an apparent attempt to jeopardize my ability to have children. I was fuming.

Minutes later, I cleared the ball from behind our net and this same bozo shouted, "Afraid to face me?" I snapped. He turned to skate away and I choked up on my stick like a baseball bat. I swung as hard as I could, like a designated hitter on performance-enhancing drugs, right at his head. Thwaaaaaap! His helmet literally spun like a top as he staggered over to the bench. His coach jumped the boards to fight me, until he realized I was a scrawny seventh grader. I shudder to think of what could have happened....

Revenge. It is the ugliest side of anger. And it happens with porn too. Angry people enjoy porn because porn is a way to swing back, to get revenge on those who have hurt us.

Think of the husband whose wife isn't that interested in sex. He tries to initiate, but she's got other things on her mind. This isn't the first time, and the record of rejection rips at his heart. *I'll show her*, he thinks as he marches off to his office. So he Googles the right words and finds the women who never say no. If his wife wonders what he's up to, all the better. Maybe she'll feel rejected like he does.

Think of the young woman who doesn't get asked to prom. Her best friend gets three invitations while she gets totally ignored. Despite her intelligence and her kindness, the guys chase the skinnier, prettier, more superficial girls. And she's angry. She takes her phone into her room and finds the kind of porn that makes her feel in control.

---

[27] Along with carpenter jeans, the Backstreet Boys, and dial-up internet.

Think of those who are simply angry at life. Those who work with demanding bosses. Those who live under the same roof as exasperating mothers. Those who sit on the bench. Those who are victims of racism. That anger simmers just beneath the surface, and porn promises a powerful release.

Thankfully, God can snuff out that sizzling wick before it blows up in irreversible impurity. Take the psalms, for example. King David wrote song after song with fists that clenched his quill. He poured out his frustration and confusion and desperation to God. He didn't stuff his emotions or sweep them under the rug. No, he brought them to God. He ran to the only refuge that could keep his soul safe. He sought peace for his troubled heart from the Prince of peace himself.

That same God is ready for our anger too. "Call on me in the day of trouble," our Father invites his angry children (Psalm 50:15). Be raw and real with God. Cry out and shout and stamp your feet. Let God deal with your anger with his promises of justice and his limitless compassion. Look to the Lord before you look to porn. Because not being Angry is the third step in enjoying sexual H.E.A.L.T.H.

## LONELY

This might sound blasphemous, but I think porn is a lot like God. Want proof? Who can make this promise and keep it? "Surely I am with you always" (Matthew 28:20). You might recognize those as Jesus' words right before his return to heaven. But doesn't porn make the same promise? In a world where the internet is in our pockets (and images are seared by epinephrine into our brains), porn is never more than two seconds away.

Which makes loneliness so dangerous. When we feel alone, porn promises to be our closest friend. When no one responds to our group text. When we are alone at home while our friends are out on dates. When you're away from your husband on a business trip. People are rooted to one GPS location at a time. But not porn. Porn is with us. Always.

Compound that with the feeling of boredom. When there's nothing to do. When you've checked your email, checked the weather, checked the channels, checked your email (again), and it's only 8:17 P.M. When there's nothing online, nothing on TV, nothing interesting on social media. But there's always something exciting on porn. Despite the dull, empty feeling that will follow, there's that predictable rush as soon as the thought of porn enters your mind.

So how do you fight feelings of loneliness and boredom? With them and with Him.

Start with them. With people. With a community. I know this can be a huge step, especially for God's introverted daughters and shy sons, but getting connected to non-pixelated people is vital to sexual purity. Could you join a book club? A sports league? A gym? A game night? A group of musicians or artists in town? Could you schedule a monthly meal with friends or join a Bible study at your church? Could you find a place or two to volunteer in your city? If idle hands are the devil's toys, what can you do to keep those hands busy with face-to-face interaction?

One of the key insights I remember from my visits with a counselor was that our brains are bad at multitasking. It is hard to engage in an activity and think about porn at the same time. My counselor encouraged me not to just sit around and wait for temptation to pass. Rather, go do something! Get the brain focused on something else. Reach out to friends, family, neighbors, anyone, and you might find yourself forgetting about porn.

Then add him. God. The God who is with you always, but, unlike porn, never leaves you with shame or regret. The God who wants to be with you to bless you, excite you, fill you, and fulfill you with peace and joy and purpose. Could you add a prayer walk to your day (ideally, right during the time you are most tempted)? Leave your devices at home and spend some time in God's creation, talking to your Father. Talk trash to the father of lies as you ask the Spirit to open your eyes to see the truth about porn. As you walk and talk, think deeply about the height and width and depth of Jesus' love for you.

I once asked a group of men to fight back against the exciting nature of porn. The youngest guy in the room, a young teenager, raised his hand. To be honest, I wasn't expecting the most mature theological answer from a kid who had never shaved. But I was wrong! He said, "Thinking about Jesus' love for us on the cross is pretty exciting, don't you think?" Yes! Preach, young man!

When my heart is bored with another day and another week and another year, I can meditate on the crazy love Jesus had when he bled and died for a sinner like me. The Holy Spirit can open the eyes of my heart to see Jesus, risen from the dead, walking with me, smiling because he delights in me, despite all my deviant thoughts (Zephaniah 3:17). Personally, I love to stop and picture God sitting in my car or on the couch in my office. And he is smiling. Always smiling. Because I am his son, and he is well pleased with me. That image reminds me that I am never alone, and I am never without the most exciting thought in the universe—I am a friend of God! That saves me from Loneliness, which is the fourth step in enjoying sexual H.E.A.L.T.H.

### TIRED

I can't find a Bible passage to prove it, but I am 94 percent sure that God doesn't count any sins that happen between 1 A.M. and 5 A.M. I have invented this teaching to comfort the parents of newborns at our church.

Because we are not the holiest people when we are tired. After our firstborn came home, I experienced the 2 A.M. rage that can only be birthed out of pure exhaustion. I would swear as our little girl screamed. In my defense, I did it in Spanish because that seemed a bit more appropriate than dropping an English f-bomb in front of a baby.[28]

Ever been there? Maybe you haven't had a newborn, but have you ever been so tired that you couldn't even remember the Ten Commandments, much less obey them?

Porn pounces on worn-out women and exhausted men. All our energy, it seems, is directed to staying conscious, instead of thinking critically about the wreckage that porn will bring. Predictably, then, porn works in a vicious cycle. You stay up late, looking for the perfect porn, and you end up with six hours of sleep. You wake up, tired (and ashamed), and make it through your day on caffeine and adrenaline, but you crash at night. Exhausted, you slump in bed, grab your device, and . . . yup, you guessed it, the hour-long, sleep-depriving search begins.

So what's the solution? I would suggest that believing in the Trinity is a good place to start. "But," you object, "I already do. I'm a Christian, after all." But do you really believe that God is the Creator of heaven and earth? Do you believe that God made all of you, your brain and body and sleep cycle included? Too often we think we can treat our bodies in a way they were not designed to be treated, like we created them ourselves. Despite the timeless wisdom that we need good food, good sleep, and good exercise, we believe we can shortcut the Creator's design. And we suffer the consequences of our foolishness in unexpected ways . . . like porn.

Yes, it is essential to fight porn with the grace of Jesus Christ (Titus 2:11). Yes, the fruit of the Holy Spirit is self-control in the face of sexual temptation (Galatians 5:23). And, yes, remembering the Father who knit your body together in your mother's womb is essential too (Psalm 139:13).

---

[28] Are you judging me at this point? Don't act like you've never sworn at a baby before.

So sleep! Put down your phone, your book, your remote, and sleep. Sleep might be the key to your sanctification! Sometimes good works don't take much work at all! Because not being Tired is the fifth step in enjoying sexual H.E.A.L.T.H.

### HEART

When a boy falls in love with a girl, he becomes irrationally infatuated. You don't have to tell him to think about her or spend time with her or invest money to prove his undying love for her. He just does. His heart is, for the moment, captivated by her love.

What's my point? Simply that out of the overflow of the heart come the works of our hands. What captures the soul controls our sanctification. The difference between selfish masturbation and selfless service, two polar opposite works of our hands, comes down to the deepest passions of the heart.

This truth is where all the psychological tips fall short. Yes, any human can choose to sleep eight hours, exercise daily, eliminate high-fructose corn syrup, and volunteer in the community. But only those who know Jesus have the explosive happiness the gospel brings to the human heart. Psalm 13:5 says, "My heart rejoices in your salvation!" Hannah, that Old Testament believer, sang, "My heart rejoices in the LORD" (1 Samuel 2:1). This isn't a going-through-the-motions ritual but an emotional relationship to God, a relationship that compels our lips and hands and feet and minds to holy living.

In fact, this is so important for the Christian life that the wisest man on earth reminded us, "Above all else, guard your heart, for everything you do flows from it" (Proverbs 4:23). Every single decision we make is directed by the passions of the heart, the center of our very being. No wonder Jesus said the most important commandment in the entire Bible was to "love the Lord your God with all your heart" (Matthew 22:37).

So how do you do that? How do you come to love God so much that your heart leads your hands (and eyes) to do holy things? My best answers to that question are nature and Scripture.

First, few things stir the heart like nature. And I don't just mean majestic mountains and a glassy lake up north. I mean the entire world around us. The smell of my daughters' hair. The beat of your favorite jam on the radio. The taste of expensive sushi or a fine scotch. The thrill of a playoff game won at the buzzer. The first deep breath when you walk outside in spring. All the exciting, beautiful moments of life.

How does that stir our hearts to love God? Because that stuff is like God! As I mentioned before, the angels cried out to the prophet Isaiah, "The whole earth is full of [the LORD's] glory" (Isaiah 6:3). The *whole* earth. Everything all around us is preaching to us, "God is a big deal! You think this is fun? Wait until you see God! You think this feels good? Wait until you are with God! You wish this moment would last forever? It will be even better when you stand before God!" The more we take all the good moments of our lives and remember that they are .00001 percent of the way we will feel when we look into the face of God, the more our hearts love God with a passion.

Second, Scripture stirs our hearts. All the steak and sushi and sports in the world could never tell us that God loves sinners like us. But Scripture does. In fact, as we have already seen, Scripture is pretty specific about God's love for sexual sinners. Abraham. Judah. David. And so many more. All the promises of grace and mercy and forgiveness and redemption and salvation and cleansing are guaranteed to everyone who believes in the name of Jesus Christ.

That is so beautifully illogical. I don't know anyone who loves me the same after I fall into sin. The expression on their faces always changes to anger and disappointment and distance. But, because of the blood Jesus shed for us on the cross, God's face is shining on us and looking on us with favor. That's why I love that ancient blessing that many churches use at the very end of worship: "The LORD bless you and keep you; the LORD make his face shine upon you and be gracious to you; the LORD turn his face toward you and give you peace" (Numbers 6:24-26). Isn't that so crazy? God's face is shining on us. After all the failures. After all the falls. After all the porn. He is pleased with us.

Let that thought stir your heart. Let grace set down roots in your heart as you meditate on passages like that. Combine that with a million little sermons nature is preaching, and your heart will be in love with God. Because guarding your Heart is the final step in sexual H.E.A.L.T.H.

### SARAH AND JUAN

I wonder what would have happened to Sarah and Juan if they had been H.E.A.L.T.H.y people. If Sarah was so thrilled with God's love that she didn't need to make another sale, get another check, and live an unbalanced life. If Juan was a man of the Word and prayer who worked through the issues in his marriage with an open Bible on the table. I realize that temptation would still exist. The evil one would still try to lure them into porn or some other sinful alternative. But they would be stronger, more resilient, more excited to honor God with their bodies.

How about you? What steps do you plan to take to become a person of better H.E.A.L.T.H.?

# The Running Man

As a man who can't say no to the dance floor, I have learned that everyone loves the Running Man.[29] Are you familiar? The

---

[29] Not to be confused with the 1987 smash hit movie *The Running Man*, where Arnold Schwarzenegger played an imprisoned game show contestant who ran to save his life. When I was seven, this movie was almost as good as *Predator*.

Macarena is cheesy. The Worm gets your wedding clothes all dirty. But the Running Man is a classic. If you ever find yourself in one of those big circles where people dance one at a time, do the Running Man and get ready for the bridesmaids to go crazy!

As a man who tries to say no to porn, I have learned that God loves running men. Are you familiar? That is when you run from sexual temptation as fast as you can. Instead of sitting around and waiting to see if you are strong enough to resist, you run from tempting situations like Usain Bolt at the Olympics.

This is what Paul told the Corinthians who lived in the shadow of Aphrodite's temple. He pleaded, "Flee from sexual immorality. All other sins a person commits are outside the body, but whoever sins sexually, sins against their own body" (1 Corinthians 6:18). In the original Greek, "sexual immorality" is the word *porneia* and "flee" is an action that is meant to be repeated. Literally, Paul is saying, "Keep fleeing from porn!" Whenever and wherever you see it, keep running away from porn.

Where do you run into porn? Are there certain websites that aren't porn but whose advertisements trigger sinful sexual thoughts? Maybe it is hard to check your fantasy football lineup on the same website that pushes Miami cheerleaders and annual swimsuit issues. Maybe you need to flee from it.

Are there certain magazines that aren't wrapped in black plastic but whose articles are the seed that blossoms into darker behavior before the day is done? I had to cancel my subscription to *Men's Health* because the ads in the back were always racy, and I needed to flee from it.

Are there certain bars or clubs that are dangerous for your heart? Hooters might have great wings, but those wings might carry your thoughts to impure places, and you need to flee from it.

Are there books that lure you into sexual lies? Romance novels are famous for making sex fictionally simple, leaving countless wives dissatisfied with the man they actually married, and you need to flee from them.

Are there TV shows whose token sex scenes take a toll on your heart? I love a good series, but sometimes I can tell by the first episode that the series will soil my soul, and I need to flee from it.

I realize this is all a bit intense. Some of these are advanced steps. But taking two giant steps back from the edge of what is technically not sinful might keep you from falling off the cliff when the winds of weakness gust through your life.

Please do not forget what we have learned—porn hurts. Porn wants to kill you. Porn plans to murder the good things that your loving Father wants to give you. Intensity about purity is never insanity.

Think of your running away like *Monty Python*. Have you seen *Monty Python and the Holy Grail*?[30] King Arthur and his brave knights have finally drawn near the cave where a hideous beast guards the grail. They scout out the scene behind rocks, waiting for a dragon or horrific monster to emerge from the smoking darkness. And then out comes . . . a rabbit. A cute, puffball-tailed, wiggly nosed rabbit.

King Arthur's men scoff at the cottontail. "What's he do, nibble your bum?" one mocks in a delightfully English accent. Grabbing his sword, the knight goes to make rabbit stew, but before he can swing, the rabbit lunges at his throat, chewing his head clean off with his "sharp pointy teeth." Arthur's army charges into battle, but the bunny strikes again, decapitating even the bravest among them, until the king finally cries, "Run away! Run away!"

---

[30] Along with *The Running Man* and *Predator*, it was one of the greatest movies of my childhood.

Porn is like that. For all the dire warnings, it seems so innocent. Just sex-positive people enjoying an escape. Just a free way to release tension. Just a safe way to explore your sexuality. But, like that little rabbit, porn devours us. It is fiercely addicting, chewing off the self-control of the most committed Christian. Therefore, we are wise to listen to King Arthur's warning. Run away!

If your experience is anything like mine, the closer you get to temptation, the harder it becomes to resist. When I stay away from Amazon and Barnes & Noble, I buy fewer books. When I skip a trip to the mall, I don't feel an urge to buy more clothes. And when I run away from sexually explicit media, I often don't even think about sexual sin. So keep fleeing from porn!

One final thought—I realize you can't run away from it all. I can't drive down the highway without seeing seven billboards for strip clubs and adult bookstores. You can't grocery shop without suggestive images at the end of every checkout aisle. We can't control how people dress at the gym or even at church.

I think of the time we took our daughters to Las Vegas.[31] We warned our little girls about the City of Sin, the billboards, and the business cards. One night we were walking down the strip, and our six-year-old said, "Dad, I saw something inappropriate, so I looked the other way. But then I saw something else inappropriate, so I looked down at my shoes. But then I saw something inappropriate on the ground, so I closed my eyes."

Ever feel like that? You are trying so hard to fix your eyes on Jesus, but sometimes there's not much to look at! You are trying to keep the covenant to not look lustfully, but you don't know how to walk down the street with your eyes open.

If you ever find yourself in that situation, let me suggest one little word that Martin Luther made famous. He once wrote

---

[31] Now you are totally judging my parenting. . . . Okay, I will admit this was a debatable decision.

that "one little word" can make the devil fall. I used to think the word was *Jesus* or *forgiven* or something connected to the gospel. But, according to my friend Jasper, the word Luther was thinking of was *liar!*[32]

So when you see and sense that temptation, when you feel the pull of the forbidden, feel free to shout, "Liar!" Rip back the curtain, and expose the enemy. Call him out. Resist him, as James encourages (James 4:7).

Personally, I like to say that out loud: "Liar!" Why in the world would I do that? Because it is my way of remembering how aggressively Satan wants to hurt me. It's a reminder that I am in a spiritual war, and there are real consequences of giving in to sexual sin. It's a graphic way of telling myself that porn will do graphic damage to my body, my marriage, my children, and my eternal soul. So yeah, I get a bit intense about porn. I want to stiff-arm it out of my sight and run away as fast as I can.

How about you? What intense steps can keep you away from the insanity of pornography?

## Awkward Steps

The baby freeze. As much as I wish I knew how to break-dance, I only really know one breaking move.[33] It is called the baby freeze, and it was super awkward to learn. Imagine holding up your entire body by putting one hand flat on the floor and then jamming your elbow into your gut. Lean forward and balance on that single hand. Go ahead, try it. Finding the right spot (two inches to the side of your belly button) and learning

---

32 I didn't fact-check this, so if this is historically inaccurate, please blame Jasper.

33 Being scrawny and unable to touch my toes are major hindrances to my plan to create the first ever pastoral breakdance crew, which I tentatively named "You Got Served (Some Jesus)!"

to balance your body weight is brutal. I got rug burns on my face trying to learn how to baby freeze. A+ for awkwardness!

I am about to suggest some of the most awkward steps to avoiding porn. Like learning how to baby freeze, these are much, much harder than eating three meals a day or unsubscribing from *Sports Illustrated*. They are so unreasonable that some of you might think they are impossible for your personal situation. But I believe they are key to helping sexual sinners in the early stages of their recovery.

**Step 1:** No isolated internet. For the vast majority of porn users, the internet leads to iniquity. A stash of magazines or hard copies of videos might tempt some, but everyone I meet tells me the internet is always the place where they find porn. Therefore, I am suggesting that some of you never use the internet alone.

This is the awkward step I took to run away from my addiction. Remember the story of the carpeted stairs? Our computer was downstairs, two floors away from my wife. When I was online, I was alone. So we decided to move the family computer upstairs, where everyone in the living room and kitchen could see it.

Not only that, but my wife put a password on the computer so I had to ask her permission to use it. That's right . . . I needed to ask my wife to log me on to the internet. Pathetic, right? Actually, no. It was one of the smartest things I did.

How about you? What if you didn't see private internet as your God-given right, but as a privilege for the self-controlled? What if you dealt with some inconvenience to avoid even graver consequences? What sort of personalized plan could you and your accountability partners create to keep you safe? Restricting your devices to public spaces? Using public WiFi instead of private data to force your internet usage into coffee shops and bookstores?

Satan loves one-on-one matchups. Therefore, refuse to isolate yourself with one of his favorite weapons.

**Step 2:** Play dumb. When Steve Jobs unveiled the iPhone in 2007, the devil was taking notes. He wasn't about to sit around and let God monopolize this innovative invention for kingdom purposes. Can you see the schemer connecting the dots? *The internet in your pocket. . . . Porn is on the internet. . . . So they will always have porn in their pockets. . . .*

Some of you know how dangerous smartphones are. They are easily taken into bathrooms behind locked doors. They are often at our bedsides, in private spaces where we are alone and tired and bored. They can be taken to sleepovers and smuggled onto playgrounds and can turn any square inch on God's green earth into an adult bookstore. You know these facts because your phone was "smart" enough to find the porn you requested. Or maybe you have kids and you fear the internet searches that happen when you are out of the room.

So what if we played dumb? What if we tried to live, as everyone has for two thousand years since Jesus' birth, without the internet in our pockets? What if we chose inconvenience over immorality? What if (be prepared to gasp) we bought a dumb phone?

Okay, I get it. I lost most of you there. That's a step way harder than the baby freeze. What about work? What about school? What about social media? What about a thousand other good things that you do on your phone? I get it. And I agree. Those are incredible perks of having the internet in your pocket. If possible, God and I would love for you to enjoy as many of those perks as possible.

But not at the expense of your purity. Imagine an alcoholic who carried a full flask in his pocket that he sipped on every other day. Would you have any sympathy for him if he pleaded with you for help with his addiction but wasn't willing to live flask-free?

Idolatry is defined as loving something more than we love God. We think of money and romance and success as American idols, but what about convenience? Are you willing to be inconvenienced if convenience is keeping you from obedience? Or has convenience kicked Christ off the throne of your heart?

I will never forget a man who ruined his life in his pursuit of short-term pleasure. I met him after his divorce as he tried to put together the pieces of his post-porn life. What made him so memorable was the intensely awkward steps he was taking—"Pastor, I want you to have the password to unlock the internet and all my apps. Any time I want to use them, I will have to come to you." Whoa. Imagine having to make a trip to see your pastor just to check the news or use Google!

But his rationale was inspiring. With the look of a man who had lost far too much, he explained, "The convenience isn't worth it." Exactly. Or, as Paul once reminded the Corinthians, "Not everything is beneficial" (1 Corinthians 6:12).

# Next Steps?

Do you know what to do next? We have covered a lot of practical ideas to reject and resist porn, but what are your next steps? Feel free to scribble them here in the margin so you don't forget. Are they embracing the blessings of H.E.A.L.T.H.? Or becoming a Running Man of God? Or rethinking your relationship with the internet? Our next steps might look a little different from one another, but I pray that you have a next step to take.

I wouldn't push you this hard if it wasn't necessary, but the devil is not known for having mercy. He is just looking for one gap in your armor to thrust the sword of sin. He couldn't care less if you keep nine of the commandments, as long as there is one that works every time. Therefore, I want to push you to make sure you are not easy prey for his plans.

A few years ago, I was staying at a La Quinta Inn while taking a class on preaching. After enjoying dinner with my classmates, I came back to my room and went straight to bed. But then I had a dream. In my dream, I was carrying a bike through this building, hoisting it up a metal staircase. I turned around and suddenly saw a topless woman, inviting me to come and talk with her. At that moment, I snapped awake in my bed, thankful it was just a dream. The temptation wasn't real, so I soon drifted back to sleep.

But then I dreamed again. This time I was running feverishly from a monstrous snake. The snake slithered after me, unhinging his massive jaws. I sprinted as fast as I could, but I wasn't fast enough. He lurched towards me, ready to devour me whole. At that moment, I snapped awake again, alone and staring at the hotel television, which was all too willing to offer content that makes Jesus Christ cry. My eyes were fixed on an opportunity to sin.

However, there was a song playing in my head. The lyrics flowed through my mind as I sat up in bed—"Christ is enough for me/Christ is enough for me/Everything I need is in you/ Everything I need."

Whoa . . . I don't put too much stock in interpreting dreams, but that was a crazy night. Hunted by the serpent, facing right-there temptation, but protected by the sufficiency of Jesus Christ.

Unfortunately, we cannot know when sin will stop crouching at our door and start pouncing at its potential prey. Thankfully, there is much we can do to prepare ourselves for that battle— next steps to help us put on the full armor of God and stand our ground. Even better, our Savior is at our side to fight for us and with us.

# Everybody Dance Now

I remember the first presentation I ever did on porn. The organizers of a men's conference invited me to speak, and I chose to dive into the topic headfirst. However, we were not sure if anyone would show up. Would the topic scare the guys away? Would they feel outed if they signed up for this breakout session? One guy later admitted that he planned to walk past the room to scope out if anyone else was there, giving him a chance to bail if he was the only attendee. I don't blame him. Can you imagine sitting alone in a room as the "Porn Pastor" makes constant eye contact?

To my surprise, however, guys showed up. Lots of them. The seats filled up and then more guys stood in the back and then even more stood out in the hallway. I told them my story and shared God's love for porn users. And I will never forget the looks on their faces. Red eyes wept back at me. In almost every row. These were dedicated Christian men who loved God and loved their church, men who hated the porn that was hurting them in so many ways.

After I wrapped up my talk, I noticed a line of guys waiting for me. One by one, they told me their stories of struggle and addiction and escape. Some shared tips. Others asked for help. All of them had something to say.

In the last five years, as I have preached and presented about pornography, I have learned, time and time again, that what happened at that conference was not the exception but the rule. God's people want to talk. They won't talk unless they know it's safe, unless they know there's compassion, unless they sense the air of grace—but they want to talk. I have come to expect to see that guy waiting for the handshakes to finish up so he can approach me with that timid look and ask the question they always ask, "Can we talk for a second?" Absolutely, brother.

So can we talk? Can we, as brothers and sisters in the faith, talk openly and compassionately and evangelically about porn? Can moms and dads talk with sons and daughters about the internet and masturbation, about the curse of porn and the blessings of grace? Can church friends talk honestly about temptation, about the messy stuff we church people do but hate to admit? Can pastors and teachers talk with compassion and candor about the sins that affect everyone in their spiritual family, either directly or indirectly?

Before this book is too far from your memory, I would love to ask you to take one simple step. I would love for you to find just one person that you love and ask them this question:

If either of us ever struggled,<br>would it be okay if we talked about porn?

You don't have to confess anything just yet. You don't have to force a conversation with the members of your family. Just ask that question. Let your significant other and your kids and your friends and your church family know that if anyone struggles with porn, this is a safe place to get help. This is a place where love is found. Our love. His love. Because love is the beat that draws us to the dance floor.

I once attended a Christian conference on porn. The speakers were passionate about the dangers of impurity. I give them credit for their courage in bringing up the issue and in sharing their own stories and struggles. However, the tone was intense. The warnings and threats were followed by more warnings and threats. I looked around at the men in the room. Their heads were hanging, their expressions cringing, as the seriousness of their sexual sin beat their joy into the cement.

But, since God has a sense of humor, a cell phone went off. An obnoxious ringtone at just the wrong time. The music pierced the heavy air in the room. The song? "Everybody Dance Now" by C&C Music Factory.[34] I am not making this up. The club beat blasted from this guy's phone. He scrambled to shut off the music, mortified at the distraction. But the guy only increased the volume as he took the device out of his pocket. He pushed every possible button, praying for an end to the agony, but before he found the power off switch, the lead singer shouted, "Everybody dance now!"

Yes! It was so beautifully awkward.[35] But after the music died down, the presenter went back to the wreckage of porn. Our smiles instantly erased, and we resumed our groveling. A few minutes later, we all shuffled out of the church, moping and not dancing.

Too often, discussing porn feels like that moment. We know it's bad. We hate it. We don't want to do it. And threats remind us just how bad we are.

But what if there is something we can say to one another, something more than "Stop it!"? What if there is a way to leave our conversations dancing, no matter how ugly our struggle? There is. Because Jesus once told a famous tale about a kid who got dirty in dozens of ways. But the boy came back to his father and learned, as every grace-loving Christian has since, that our dirty won't stop God from dancing.

When he came near the house,
he heard music and dancing.

(LUKE 15:25)

---

[34] C&C Music Factory was recently ranked the #2 greatest band of the 1990s, losing a close vote to Ace of Base.

[35] Ironically, this guy shows up at my church from time to time, so I'm waiting for the ringtone during one of my sermons.